Kingdom of Saudi Arabia

Cultural Awareness and

Business Negotiations

Country Study

Contents

INTRODUCTION

In our increasingly interconnected world, understanding and embracing cultural diversity has become essential for both personal and professional success. This series of Cultural Awareness books aims to provide participants with the knowledge, skills, and tools necessary to better understand and navigate various cultural contexts. By investing in cultural awareness, we are not only fostering stronger relationships but also paving the way for more successful business ventures and personal growth.

The expanding Global market presents immense opportunities for businesses. However, these opportunities come with the responsibility of understanding the nuances of various cultures. Unintentional cultural misunderstandings can jeopardise your chances of securing a crucial foothold in this lucrative market. This series highlights the importance of being aware of cultural differences and equips you with the tools to deal with the challenges that may arise when interacting with individuals from different cultural backgrounds.

Individuals and families who have travelled or are planning to move to different countries also face the challenge of adapting to new cultures. Culture shock can be overwhelming if one is not prepared to handle the changes that come with relocating. This course offers practical insights and tools to help individuals and families better understand and navigate the complexities of their new cultural environment.

Cultural awareness goes beyond learning facts or memorizing customs; it is about cultivating a genuine appreciation for the richness of human experiences. This series encourages participants to look beyond their own cultural lens and develop empathy for the perspectives of others. By doing so, we foster a more inclusive and harmonious world where people from diverse backgrounds can come together and create meaningful connections.

Throughout this book, you will be introduced to various cultural frameworks, practices, and traditions, as well as common misconceptions and stereotypes that often contribute to misunderstandings and miscommunications. Engaging with these topics will enable you to recognise cultural differences, appreciate their value, and navigate them effectively.

In conclusion, cultural awareness is essential for anyone aiming to expand their reach in the global market, adapt to new cultural environments, or enrich their lives by embracing the beauty of human diversity. By undertaking this journey, you are taking a significant step toward creating a more inclusive, empathetic, and successful future.

Ask yourself: Can you afford to miss out on the vital opportunities and personal growth that cultural awareness can bring to your life? The time to invest in cultural understanding is now. Welcome to an enlightening and transformative journey.

1. WHAT IS CULTURE?

What is Culture?

The Culture of a people can be understood as the system of shared ideas and meanings, explicit and implicit, which a people use to interpret the world, and which serve to pattern their behaviour.

This includes an understanding of the art, literature, and history of a society, but also less tangible aspects such as attitudes, prejudices, folklore etc. Unconscious or conscious habits are just as important as art and history.

<u>Values</u> - What people say one ought to do or not do? What is considered good or bad - the importance of honesty, or chastity?

<u>Laws</u> - What political authorities have decided people should do, and what the sanctions are?

<u>Rules</u> - What a society has decided its members should do. Social rules about marriage ages, childrearing.

<u>Social Categories</u>- Ways of thinking about people as types. - "friends", "criminals", "lovers", "nobles", "clergy".

<u>Tacit Models</u> - Implicit standards and patterns of behaviour that a person does not think about - knowing how to address a police officer rather than friends. Knowing how to dress for a job interview as opposed to a dance.

<u>Fundamental</u> - Categories and ways of thinking that people take for granted and may not recognise even when pointed out. - thinking in dualities good/bad, male/female.

Culture shapes

- The way we think.
- The way we interact.
- The way we communicate.
- The way we transmit knowledge to the next generation.

Culture manifests itself in

- Food
- Religion
- Dress
- Differences in language
- Our expectations of male and female roles
- Non-verbal rules and body language

The first step is in understanding the values and rules for behaviour of our own culture - the "normal" or "right" way of doing things. What makes us different?

Geert Hofstede

Between 1967 and 1973 Geert Hofstede conducted a study on culture across 100 000 employees of IBM in 50 countries. From this he developed a framework to 'measure' the 'value dimensions' of various cultures.

Hofstede identified f values which can be related to each culture:

- Individualism
- Masculinity
- Power Distance, and
- Uncertainty Avoidance

Later studies by Trompenaar have added several more; however, I will address the 4 basic values along with one later addition relating to time.

From surveys, Hofstede was able to map the cultures and compare them, and from this extrapolate as to why a culture may act in a particular way.

Taking the basic values separately, measured on a scale of 0 to 100.

	PD	ID	M	UA	LT
AUS	38M	90H	61H	51M	21L
KSA	72H	48M	43M	64H	27L
USA	40	91	62	46	26
UK	35	89	66	35	51

H = top third of countries

M = medium

L = bottom third

Power Distance

The Hofstede Power Distance dimension refers to the way cultures perceive and handle inequalities within their societies. In the context of Saudi Arabia, the Power Distance dimension is particularly relevant due to the country's high score of **72**, which indicates a strong acceptance of hierarchical order and unequal distribution of power.

In Saudi Arabian culture, this high Power Distance score suggests that individuals readily accept the existence of a hierarchical structure in various aspects of their lives, including family, social, and professional environments. People believe that everyone has a designated place within this hierarchy, and they do not question or challenge this order.

In organizations, the high Power Distance in Saudi Arabia translates to a centralized decision-making process, with power and authority concentrated at the top levels of management. Subordinates expect to be given clear instructions and generally do not question or criticize their superiors' decisions. The ideal leader in this context is seen as a benevolent authoritarian, who exerts firm control while also showing concern and care for their subordinates.

This cultural preference for hierarchical order and acceptance of power inequalities in Saudi Arabia can be attributed to various factors, including the country's historical, religious, and social influences. The strong presence of Islamic traditions and values, combined with the monarchy system, contribute to the high regard for authority and the importance of respecting one's position within the societal hierarchy.

It is crucial for individuals and businesses interacting with Saudi Arabian culture to understand and respect this high Power Distance dimension. To effectively communicate and collaborate, one must be aware of the cultural norms and expectations regarding hierarchy, authority, and the roles of superiors and subordinates in both professional and social settings.

Individualism v. Collectivism

This dimension aims to measure the degree of interdependence among members of a society and how they define their self-image.

In **individualistic** societies:

- People prioritize their personal goals, needs, and achievements over those of their social groups.
- Independence and self-reliance are highly valued, and people are encouraged to express their individual opinions and preferences.
- Personal success and accomplishments are celebrated, and competition is often seen as a driving force for progress.
- Relationships tend to be more flexible, and people have the freedom to choose their own social circles and affiliations.
- The primary responsibility of individuals is to take care of themselves and their immediate family members.

In **collectivist** societies:

- The welfare of the group is placed above individual interests, and people are expected to contribute to the success and well-being of their social groups.
- Interdependence and cooperation are highly valued, and individuals are expected to conform to the norms and expectations of their group.
- Social harmony and group cohesion are prioritized, with conflict resolution often focused on finding a compromise that benefits the group as a whole.
- Relationships tend to be more stable, and people are born into strong, tight-knit social groups that provide support and protection throughout their lives.
- Loyalty to one's 'in-group' is paramount, and individuals are expected to prioritize the needs of their group over their own.

The distinction between individualism and collectivism reflects the ways in which societies balance individual autonomy and group harmony. It is important to note that these dimensions are not mutually exclusive; rather, they represent a spectrum along which different cultures fall. Understanding these cultural differences can help in navigating cross-cultural communication and collaboration effectively.

The Individualism dimension in Hofstede's framework measures the extent to which a society values individual achievements and personal autonomy over group cohesion and collective goals. A high score in Individualism indicates a preference for individualism, while a low score indicates a preference for collectivism.

In the context of Saudi Arabia, the country scores lower on the Individualism dimension, reflecting a predominantly collectivist culture. This means that Saudi Arabian society places a strong emphasis on the importance of groups, such as family, extended family, and other social networks. Individuals are expected to prioritize the well-being and interests of these groups over their personal ambitions and desires.

In a collectivist culture like Saudi Arabia, loyalty to one's family and social groups is highly valued, and interpersonal relationships play a significant role in both personal and professional settings. People tend to rely on their connections for support, guidance, and problem-solving. Decisions are often made with the group's interests in mind, and maintaining harmony within the group is considered essential.

In professional settings, managers in Saudi Arabia often take a more paternalistic approach, with the expectation that employees will show loyalty and commitment to the organization. In return, the organization is expected to look after the employees' needs and welfare. This emphasis on loyalty and group harmony influences the way businesses operate, negotiate, and build relationships in Saudi Arabia.

For individuals and businesses engaging with Saudi Arabian culture, it is important to understand and respect the low individualism score and the collectivist nature of the society. Effective communication and collaboration require an awareness of the cultural norms and expectations surrounding group dynamics, interpersonal relationships, and the importance of loyalty and harmony within social and professional networks.

Overall, the KSA collectivist culture emphasises the importance of strong relationships, loyalty, and group harmony. These values are deeply ingrained in various aspects of society, from family life to workplace dynamics.

Masculinity v. Femininity

This dimension measures the dominant values in a society and the extent to which they prioritize competition, achievement, and material success (masculine) versus caring for others, quality of life, and work-life balance (feminine).

With a score of **43** in the Masculinity versus Femininity dimension of Hofstede's framework, Saudi Arabia leans towards a more balanced approach between masculinity and femininity. However, it is essential to consider the specific cultural context and nuances that influence the society's values and gender roles.

In Saudi Arabia, the culture is strongly influenced by Islamic traditions and values, which play a significant role in defining societal expectations and norms for both men and women. As a result, Saudi Arabia has certain unique characteristics that may not be fully captured by the Masculinity versus Femininity dimension score.

A score of 43 suggests that Saudi Arabian society has elements of both masculine and feminine values. Masculine values may be seen in the importance placed on achievement, competitiveness, and assertiveness, especially in the professional realm. This can be observed in the predominantly male-dominated workforce and the traditional gender roles assigned to men as providers and leaders.

On the other hand, feminine values, such as nurturing, cooperation, and empathy, are also present in Saudi Arabian society. The strong emphasis on family and relationships reflects these feminine values. Moreover, in recent years, there has been a gradual shift towards greater gender equality, with more women participating in the workforce and taking on leadership roles.

In a society with mixed Masculine and Feminine values like KSA, you may observe the following:

In summary, with an intermediate score in the Masculinity vs. Femininity dimension, KSA culture may display a blend of both competitive and nurturing values. This can lead to a diverse and adaptable society, where people's motivations and priorities can vary depending on the situation and individual preferences.

Uncertainty Avoidance

This dimension reflects the extent to which a society feels threatened by ambiguity or uncertain situations and the strategies they use to cope with this anxiety.

With a score of **64** in the Uncertainty Avoidance dimension of Hofstede's framework, Saudi Arabia exhibits a relatively high preference for avoiding uncertainty and ambiguity. This indicates that Saudi Arabian society has a strong inclination towards maintaining stability, adhering to rules and regulations, and seeking predictability in various aspects of life.

Uncertainty Avoidance in Saudi Arabia is primarily driven by cultural, religious, and historical factors. The influence of Islamic teachings, which emphasize the importance of order and following religious guidelines, contributes to the high Uncertainty Avoidance score.

In practical terms, this score means that people in Saudi Arabia are likely to appreciate clear rules, well-defined structures, and detailed plans in both personal and professional settings. They may be risk-averse and prefer sticking to tried-and-tested methods rather than experimenting with new ideas. This preference for stability can also manifest in a strong adherence to cultural norms and traditions, as well as a general reluctance to deviate from established practices.

In a professional context, the high Uncertainty Avoidance score implies that Saudi Arabian organizations may have a more bureaucratic structure, with formalized procedures and hierarchies. Employees may seek clear instructions and guidance from their superiors and feel more comfortable when roles and expectations are explicitly defined. Innovation and change may be approached with caution, and decision-making processes could be slower, with a focus on gathering extensive information and minimizing risks.

For individuals and businesses engaging with Saudi Arabian society, understanding, and respecting the country's high Uncertainty Avoidance score is crucial for effective communication and collaboration. Recognizing the cultural preference for stability, predictability, and adherence to rules can help navigate the complexities of the Saudi Arabian cultural landscape and build strong relationships with local partners.

Long Term Orientation

With a score of 27 in the Long Term Orientation dimension of Hofstede's framework, Saudi Arabia demonstrates a relatively low preference for long-term planning and a more significant focus on maintaining traditional values and the present or short-term perspective.

A low Long Term Orientation score implies that Saudi Arabian society places a strong emphasis on preserving cultural norms, traditions, and practices. This is deeply rooted in the country's history and the influence of Islamic teachings, which play a significant role in shaping societal values and behaviours.

In practical terms, this low score means that people in Saudi Arabia may be more inclined to focus on immediate concerns and prioritize short-term gains and results. They may place a higher value on quick decision-making, respect for tradition, and adherence to established practices. The emphasis on the present can also manifest in a keen sense of loyalty to family, social networks, and religious principles.

In a professional context, the low Long Term Orientation score suggests that Saudi Arabian organizations may prioritize immediate results, rapid decision-making, and established practices over long-term planning and strategic foresight. This could also impact the approach to innovation, with a preference for incremental improvements over radical or disruptive changes.

For individuals and businesses engaging with Saudi Arabian society, understanding, and respecting the country's low Long Term Orientation score is essential for effective communication and collaboration. Recognizing the cultural preference for maintaining traditions, focusing on the present, and valuing short-term gains can help navigate the complexities of the Saudi Arabian cultural landscape and build strong relationships with local partners. Adaptability and sensitivity to the local cultural norms and values are crucial for successfully working with Saudi Arabian counterparts.

Acculturation

Acculturation is the process of adapting to a new culture.

- Variables affecting Acculturation.
- The amount of time spent in the process – educating yourself.
- The quantity and quality of interaction – trying things.
- Ethnicity or nation of origin – how far is it removed from our own.
- Affinity – willingness to learn and adapt.

Stages of Acculturation

- Acceptance of new culture - honeymoon
- Individual starts to feel comfortable in the new culture.
- Feelings of anger, hostility, and frustration
- Recovery
- Culture Shock

Generalisations

We should remember that there will probably never be one person within a culture that actually meets these dimensions. Rather this is a tool to anticipate likely reaction of a particular culture. There is never an average person! What should be remembered is that between the extremes, patterns do exist.

The inverse also applies; do not confuse a particular individual's personality as representative of culture. Whilst Australian's are considered sports loving people, there are people who don't like Rugby – as hard as that is to believe!

Stereotyping – setting a standard idea, concept or form. This 'notion' has a deeper meaning to our basic survival instincts.

Bias – a particular tendency or preference, which may prevent unprejudiced consideration of a topic. A 'learned' response.

Prejudice - an unfavourable opinion formed beforehand or without knowledge or reason.

Linear and Circular Thinking

How does culture affect Management?

Our Western (Greek) method of teaching & learning is if there is a problem then I can solve it. We are taught to identify issues as a 'problem' that challenges us. The individual works out a plan and overcomes the problem.

In a culture not rooted in Western traditions, the issue may not be seen as a 'problem'!! Rather it is a divergence or even a side issue that can be avoided or not confronted until a solution is evident.

Managing Across Culture

The management theory of MBI (Mapping – Bridging – Integrating) was developed to understand the differences and work out optimum paths to achieve greater workflows.

2. UNDERSTANDING CULTURAL AWARENESS IN SAUDI ARABIA

Cultural awareness is an essential skill for anyone seeking to engage with people from diverse backgrounds, especially when traveling, working, or living in a foreign country. In the context of Saudi Arabia, a nation with a rich cultural heritage and deeply rooted traditions, developing cultural awareness becomes even more important. This introduction aims to highlight the significance of cultural awareness in Saudi Arabia and set the stage for the exploration of various aspects of its society and customs throughout this book.

Saudi Arabia is an influential country in the Middle East, known for its vast oil reserves, religious significance as the birthplace of Islam, and its unique cultural identity. Understanding the nuances of Saudi Arabian culture is crucial for anyone seeking to establish meaningful connections, conduct business, or simply experience the country's rich heritage while visiting.

Cultural awareness involves recognizing and respecting the beliefs, values, customs, and social norms that shape the identity of a group or nation. In Saudi Arabia, the significance of cultural awareness is heightened by the nation's deeply ingrained values, which are rooted in Islamic teachings and Arab traditions. These values influence every aspect of daily life, from social interactions and family dynamics to business practices and communication styles.

By developing cultural awareness, one can.

- Enhance cross-cultural communication: Understanding the norms, customs, and etiquette of Saudi Arabian culture can help facilitate effective communication and prevent misunderstandings.
- Foster respect and mutual understanding: Being aware of cultural differences and demonstrating sensitivity to local customs can help build trust and rapport with Saudi Arabians, fostering positive relationships.
- Navigate social and business situations with confidence: Knowing what to expect in various social and professional contexts can help individuals feel more at ease and navigate situations with greater confidence.
- Contribute to a positive image of one's home country: Demonstrating cultural awareness and respect for local customs can leave a positive impression on Saudi Arabians and promote a favorable image of the visitor's home country.
- Facilitate successful business dealings: Understanding the nuances of Saudi Arabian business culture can help in negotiations, forming partnerships, and ultimately achieving success in business endeavors.

This book aims to provide a comprehensive guide to understanding the culture and customs of Saudi Arabia, covering topics such as history, religion, social norms, etiquette, communication, business practices, and more. By exploring these topics, readers will be better equipped to navigate the complexities of Saudi Arabian society, fostering meaningful connections and gaining a deeper appreciation of this fascinating country.

3. COUNTRY OVERVIEW

Brief History

Saudi Arabia is a country rich in history and cultural heritage, deeply rooted in the Arabian Peninsula's ancient civilizations and religious traditions. This section provides a brief overview of the history of Saudi Arabia, highlighting key events and developments that have shaped its identity and culture.

Pre-Islamic Period (circa 1000 BCE - 610 CE)

The Arabian Peninsula has been inhabited for thousands of years, with evidence of early human settlements dating back to prehistoric times. Ancient civilizations such as the Dilmun, Thamud, and Nabateans left their mark on the region, establishing trade routes and contributing to the development of early Arab culture. The pre-Islamic period in the Arabian Peninsula is characterized by a mix of tribal societies, city-states, and kingdoms, with local cultures influenced by neighboring civilizations such as the Egyptians, Persians, and Romans.

Birth of Islam and the Islamic Caliphates (610 - 1258 CE)

The birth of Islam in the early 7th century CE marked a turning point in the history of the Arabian Peninsula. The Prophet Muhammad, born in Mecca, received divine revelations that would later form the Islamic holy book, the Quran. Through his teachings, the new monotheistic religion of Islam rapidly spread across the region, uniting various tribes and city-states under a common religious and political system. After the death of the Prophet Muhammad, the Rashidun, Umayyad, and Abbasid Caliphates expanded the Islamic empire, consolidating Arab rule and spreading Islamic culture across a vast territory stretching from the Iberian Peninsula to India.

Fragmentation and Local Dynasties (13th - 18th centuries)

Following the decline of the Abbasid Caliphate, the Arabian Peninsula witnessed a period of fragmentation and the emergence of local dynasties. The region was divided among various tribes, city-states, and smaller kingdoms, such as the Hejaz and the Najd. The Arabian Peninsula also faced invasions and incursions from external powers, such as the Mongols, the Mamluks, and the Ottoman Empire.

Founding of the First and Second Saudi States (1744 - 1891)

The modern history of Saudi Arabia begins with the formation of the First Saudi State in the mid-18th century. The state was founded by Muhammad ibn Saud, who joined forces with a religious reformer named Muhammad ibn Abd al-Wahhab, whose teachings would later form the basis of the conservative Sunni Islamic doctrine known as Wahhabism. The First Saudi State expanded rapidly but was ultimately defeated by the Ottoman Empire and its Egyptian vassal. The Second Saudi State emerged in the 19th century but faced internal divisions and external challenges, eventually collapsing in the late 1800s.

Formation of the Kingdom of Saudi Arabia (1902 - present)

In the early 20th century, Abdulaziz ibn Saud, a descendant of the founder of the First Saudi State, embarked on a campaign to unite the Arabian Peninsula under his rule. After successfully capturing Riyadh, Abdulaziz ibn Saud established the modern Kingdom of Saudi Arabia in 1932. The discovery of vast oil reserves in the 1930s transformed the kingdom's economy and global standing. Saudi Arabia has since emerged as a leading regional power and an influential player in the Islamic world, with its economy heavily reliant on oil exports and its political system characterized by an absolute monarchy that upholds the principles of Wahhabi Islam.

Geography

Saudi Arabia is a vast country located in the Middle East, occupying most of the Arabian Peninsula. Its unique geography has played a significant role in shaping its history, culture, and economy. This section provides a brief overview of the geography of Saudi Arabia, highlighting key features and characteristics that define its landscape.

Size and Borders

Saudi Arabia is the largest country in the Middle East and the 13th largest in the world, covering an area of approximately 2.15 million square kilometers (830,000 square miles). It shares borders with eight countries: Jordan and Iraq to the north, Kuwait to the northeast, Qatar, Bahrain, and the United Arab Emirates to the east, Oman to the southeast, and Yemen to the south. To the west, Saudi Arabia has a long coastline along the Red Sea, and to the east, it has a shorter coastline along the Persian Gulf.

Topography

The topography of Saudi Arabia is characterized by diverse landscapes that include vast deserts, mountain ranges, and coastal plains. The central and eastern parts of the country are dominated by the Arabian Desert, which consists of several sub-regions, including the Rub' al-Khali (Empty Quarter) – the largest continuous sand desert in the world. The western region features the Hejaz and Asir mountain ranges, which run parallel to the Red Sea coast and reach elevations of over 3,000 meters (9,840 feet). The coastal plains along the Red Sea and the Persian Gulf are narrow, with fertile land and important agricultural regions, such as the Al-Hasa Oasis in the east.

Climate

Saudi Arabia has a predominantly arid climate, characterized by extreme heat during the day, cooler temperatures at night, and very low annual rainfall. The country experiences wide temperature fluctuations between its various regions, with average summer temperatures ranging from 42°C (108°F) in the central deserts to 30°C (86°F) in the coastal areas. In the winter, temperatures can drop to near freezing in the northern regions, while coastal areas remain relatively mild. The western highlands have a more moderate climate, with cooler temperatures and higher rainfall due to their elevation.

Natural Resources

Saudi Arabia is blessed with abundant natural resources, most notably its vast reserves of oil and natural gas. The country is the world's largest exporter of petroleum and holds around 18% of the world's proven oil reserves. In addition to hydrocarbons, Saudi Arabia has significant deposits of minerals, such as gold, copper, phosphate, and bauxite. The country's limited water resources are primarily derived from underground aquifers and desalination plants along the coast.

Environment and Wildlife

Saudi Arabia's diverse landscapes support a variety of plant and animal species adapted to the harsh desert environment. The country is home to over 2,000 plant species, many of which are endemic to the region. Animal species found in Saudi Arabia include the Arabian oryx, Nubian ibex, sand gazelle, and Arabian leopard. The country's coastal waters support a rich marine ecosystem, with coral reefs, sea turtles, and numerous fish species. Saudi Arabia faces several environmental challenges, such as desertification, water scarcity, and loss of biodiversity due to habitat destruction and overgrazing.

This geographical overview provides a snapshot of Saudi Arabia's unique landscape, highlighting the diverse features that have shaped its history, culture, and economy. The country's vast deserts, towering mountains, and rich natural resources have played a crucial role in defining its identity and continue to influence its development in the modern era.

Demographics

Saudi Arabia is a diverse and rapidly growing country, with a unique demographic landscape that has been shaped by its history, geography, and economic development. This section provides a brief overview of the demographics of Saudi Arabia, highlighting key aspects such as population size, age distribution, ethnic composition, and languages spoken.

Population Size

Saudi Arabia has a population of approximately 35 million people, making it the largest country in the Arabian Peninsula and the 40th most populous country in the world. The population has experienced rapid growth in recent decades due to a high birth rate, low mortality rate, and a significant influx of foreign workers. The country's population is heavily concentrated in urban areas, with approximately 84% of the population living in cities.

Age Distribution

The population of Saudi Arabia is relatively young, with a median age of around 31 years. Approximately 60% of the population is under the age of 30, while only 5% are over the age of 65. This young and growing population presents both opportunities and challenges for the country, as it seeks to create jobs, provide education, and build infrastructure to meet the needs of its people.

Ethnic Composition

The majority of Saudi Arabia's population is of Arab descent, with ethnic Saudis comprising around 90% of the total population. The remaining 10% consists of various ethnic minority groups, including Afro-Arabs, South Asians, Southeast Asians, and Western expatriates. The presence of a large expatriate population, which makes up approximately one-third of the total population, reflects the country's reliance on foreign labor to support its economy, particularly in sectors such as oil production, construction, and domestic services.

Languages Spoken

Arabic is the official language of Saudi Arabia and is spoken by most of the population. The Saudi dialect of Arabic, known as Najdi Arabic, is widely spoken across the country, while the Hejazi dialect is more common in the western region. Many expatriate workers in Saudi Arabia speak their native languages, such as Urdu, Bengali, Tagalog, and English. English is widely used in business and is taught as a second language in schools.

Religion

Islam is the official religion of Saudi Arabia, and the country is the birthplace of Islam and the site of its holiest cities, Mecca and Medina. Most of the population adheres to the Sunni branch of Islam, with the conservative Wahhabi doctrine being the dominant form of Sunni Islam practiced in the country. There is also a small Shia Muslim minority, primarily concentrated in the Eastern Province. The government enforces a strict policy of religious uniformity, and the practice of non-Muslim religions is not allowed in public.

4. POLITICAL AND ECONOMIC LANDSCAPE

Government Structure

Saudi Arabia is an absolute monarchy, with a unique political and economic structure that is deeply rooted in its history, culture, and religious traditions. This section provides a brief overview of the government structure of Saudi Arabia, highlighting key aspects such as the role of the monarchy, the division of powers, and the main institutions involved in governance and decision-making.

Monarchy

The King of Saudi Arabia holds the ultimate authority in the country and serves as both the head of state and the head of government. The monarchy is hereditary, with the King being a member of the House of Saud, the ruling royal family. The King's powers are extensive and include the ability to enact laws, appoint and dismiss government officials, and oversee the country's defence and foreign policy. The current King, Salman bin Abdulaziz Al Saud, ascended to the throne in January 2015.

Council of Ministers

The Council of Ministers, also known as the Cabinet, is the main executive body in Saudi Arabia and is responsible for implementing the King's decisions and overseeing the administration of the country. The Council is composed of around 30 ministers, who are appointed by the King and hold various portfolios, such as finance, defence, health, and education. The King also serves as the Prime Minister, while the Crown Prince, currently Mohammed bin Salman, serves as the Deputy Prime Minister.

Consultative Assembly

The Consultative Assembly, or Majlis al-Shura, is an advisory body that provides a limited form of representative government in Saudi Arabia. The Assembly is composed of 150 members, who are appointed by the King for four-year terms. The role of the Consultative Assembly is primarily to review and provide recommendations on laws and policies proposed by the King and the Council of Ministers. While the Assembly does not have legislative powers, its advice is considered influential in shaping the government's decisions.

Provincial and Local Government

Saudi Arabia is divided into 13 administrative regions, which are further subdivided into governorates and sub-governorates. The regional governors are appointed by the King and hold significant authority in overseeing the administration of their respective regions. Local government is organized through municipal councils, which are partially elected and partially appointed. These councils are responsible for managing local affairs, such as infrastructure development, public services, and urban planning.

Economic Landscape

Saudi Arabia's economy is heavily dependent on the production and export of petroleum, which accounts for approximately 90% of the country's export earnings and 40% of its GDP. The government plays a central role in managing the economy, with state-owned enterprises, such as Saudi Aramco, dominating key sectors. In recent years, the government has launched ambitious economic reform initiatives, such as Vision 2030, aimed at diversifying the economy, reducing reliance on oil, and fostering the growth of the private sector.

Key Leaders

Saudi Arabia's political and economic landscape is largely influenced by its key leaders, who hold significant power and authority in shaping the country's policies, governance, and development. This section provides a brief overview of the most influential leaders in Saudi Arabia, focusing on their roles, responsibilities, and impact on the country's political and economic affairs.

King Salman bin Abdulaziz Al Saud

As the current King of Saudi Arabia, King Salman is the ultimate authority in the country and holds extensive powers in enacting laws, appointing, and dismissing government officials, and overseeing the country's defence and foreign policy. Since ascending to the throne in 2015, King Salman has overseen several significant reforms, including the announcement of the ambitious Vision 2030 plan and the appointment of his son, Mohammed bin Salman, as Crown Prince.

Crown Prince Mohammed bin Salman (MbS)

As the Crown Prince and Deputy Prime Minister, Mohammed bin Salman is widely regarded as the driving force behind many of the recent political, economic, and social reforms in Saudi Arabia. MbS has championed the Vision 2030 plan, which aims to diversify the economy, reduce reliance on oil, and modernize the country's social and cultural landscape. Additionally, he has played a significant role in shaping Saudi Arabia's foreign policy, including the country's involvement in the Yemen conflict and the ongoing diplomatic dispute with Qatar.

Khalid Al-Falih

Khalid Al-Falih is a prominent figure in the Saudi Arabian government and has held several key positions, including the Minister of Energy, Industry and Mineral Resources, and the Chairman of Saudi Aramco, the state-owned oil company. Al-Falih has been instrumental in implementing economic reforms and overseeing major infrastructure projects, such as the development of new industrial cities and the expansion of the country's renewable energy capacity.

Adel Al-Jubeir

Adel Al-Jubeir is a veteran diplomat who has served as Saudi Arabia's Foreign Minister and is currently the Minister of State for Foreign Affairs. Al-Jubeir is an influential figure in shaping Saudi Arabia's foreign policy and has been involved in managing the country's relations with key international partners, such as the United States, the European Union, and other Gulf Cooperation Council (GCC) countries.

Mohammed Al-Jadaan

As the Minister of Finance, Mohammed Al-Jadaan is responsible for managing Saudi Arabia's fiscal policy and overseeing the implementation of economic reforms aimed at diversifying the economy and reducing the budget deficit. Al-Jadaan has played a crucial role in introducing various fiscal measures, such as the implementation of value-added tax (VAT) and the introduction of new public-private partnership models for infrastructure projects.

Economic Sectors

Saudi Arabia's economy is one of the largest in the Middle East and is heavily dependent on the production and export of petroleum. However, under the ambitious Vision 2030 plan, the country is working to diversify its economy and reduce its reliance on oil. The following are the key economic sectors in Saudi Arabia:

Oil and Gas

The oil and gas sector is the backbone of the Saudi Arabian economy, with petroleum accounting for approximately 90% of the country's export earnings and 40% of its GDP. Saudi Arabia is the world's largest oil exporter, and the state-owned oil company, Saudi Aramco, is the world's most valuable company. This sector has a significant impact on the country's overall economic performance and government revenues.

Petrochemicals and Mining

Saudi Arabia is rich in mineral resources, and the petrochemicals and mining sector plays a vital role in its economic diversification efforts. The country is the world's largest producer of ammonia, urea, and ethylene, and it has significant reserves of minerals like phosphate, bauxite, and gold. The Saudi Arabian government has been investing in the development of its mining sector, aiming to increase its contribution to the GDP and create new employment opportunities.

Infrastructure and Construction

As part of the Vision 2030 plan, the Saudi Arabian government has been investing heavily in infrastructure development, including transportation, housing, and urban planning projects. Major ongoing projects include the Riyadh Metro, the Jeddah Economic City, and the King Abdullah Economic City. The construction sector plays a critical role in supporting economic growth and generating employment opportunities.

Finance and Banking

The financial services sector in Saudi Arabia is well-developed, with a diverse range of banking and financial institutions, including commercial banks, Islamic banks, and investment firms. The Saudi Arabian Monetary Authority (SAMA) is the central bank and regulatory authority for the financial sector. The country's stock exchange, the Tadawul, is the largest in the Middle East and has been opening up to foreign investors in recent years.

Tourism and Hospitality

Tourism is an emerging sector in Saudi Arabia, with the government aiming to develop it as a significant source of revenue and employment under the Vision 2030 plan. The country has a rich cultural and religious heritage, with sites like Mecca and Medina attracting millions of Muslim pilgrims each year. The government is also investing in the development of leisure tourism, including the Red Sea Project and the Qiddiya entertainment city.

Retail and E-commerce

The retail sector in Saudi Arabia has been growing rapidly, driven by a growing consumer base, high disposable incomes, and increasing urbanization. The e-commerce market is also expanding, with an increasing number of consumers opting for online shopping. The government has been supporting the growth of the retail and e-commerce sectors through regulatory reforms and infrastructure investments.

5. SOCIETY AND CULTURE

Family Structure

Family holds a central position in Saudi Arabian society and culture, with family values, loyalty, and unity being highly esteemed. The family structure in Saudi Arabia is typically characterized by the following features:

Extended Family System

Saudi Arabian families often follow an extended family system, where multiple generations live together or in close proximity. This system is rooted in Islamic and Arab traditions and emphasizes the importance of strong family bonds, cooperation, and mutual support among family members. Grandparents, parents, children, and siblings often have close relationships and maintain frequent contact.

Patriarchal Structure

The family structure in Saudi Arabia is predominantly patriarchal, with the father or the eldest male being the head of the family. He is responsible for making important decisions, providing financial support, and ensuring the overall well-being of the family. This patriarchal system is deeply rooted in Saudi Arabian culture and reflects the conservative and religious values of the society.

Gender Roles

Traditional gender roles are still prevalent in Saudi Arabian families, with men primarily responsible for providing financial support and women in charge of managing the household and taking care of the children. However, with the ongoing social and economic reforms, women's participation in the workforce has been increasing, leading to a gradual shift in gender roles and expectations.

Importance of Marriage and Children

Marriage is considered an essential part of life in Saudi Arabian culture, and having children is seen as a natural progression after marriage. Arranged marriages are still common, and families play a significant role in choosing suitable spouses for their children. The concept of large families is valued, and having multiple children is a sign of prosperity and social standing.

Respect for Elders

In Saudi Arabian families, respect for elders is an essential aspect of the culture. Children are taught to show respect, obedience, and deference to their parents and older relatives. Elders are considered to be the source of wisdom and guidance, and their opinions and advice are highly regarded.

Family Events and Gatherings

Saudi Arabian families place significant importance on socializing and spending time together. Family gatherings, including dinners and special occasions, are an essential part of the culture. These events help strengthen family bonds and provide an opportunity for relatives to connect, share news, and celebrate their traditions and values.

Gender Roles

Gender roles in Saudi Arabian society have traditionally been clearly defined and influenced by Islamic teachings and cultural norms. However, in recent years, there has been a gradual shift in gender roles due to ongoing social and economic reforms. Here's an overview of gender roles in Saudi Arabia:

Traditional Gender Roles

Traditionally, adults in Saudi Arabian society have distinct roles and responsibilities. Men have been primarily responsible for providing financial support to the family and making important decisions, while women have been in charge of managing the household, raising children, and maintaining family traditions. This strict division of labor has been deeply rooted in the country's conservative and religious values.

Segregation of Genders

In line with traditional gender roles, Saudi Arabian society has practiced strict gender segregation in public spaces, with separate areas designated for people in places like restaurants, banks, and public transportation. This segregation has also been enforced in educational and professional environments, with separate institutions for people and limited interaction between the sexes.

Women's Rights and Reforms

In recent years, Saudi Arabia has witnessed significant social and legal reforms aimed at improving women's rights and opportunities. Some notable reforms include granting women the right to vote and run for office in municipal elections, allowing women to drive, and lifting the requirement for a male guardian's permission for women to travel, work, or access healthcare services. These reforms have contributed to a gradual shift in gender roles and expectations, with more women entering the workforce, pursuing higher education, and participating in public life.

Changing Gender Roles

As a result of the ongoing reforms, gender roles in Saudi Arabian society are slowly evolving. Women's participation in the workforce has been steadily increasing, and they are now represented in various fields, including education, healthcare, finance, and technology. Furthermore, with more women pursuing higher education, the traditional expectations of women focusing solely on family life are being challenged.

Balancing Tradition and Modernity

Despite these changes, traditional gender roles and expectations still persist in many aspects of Saudi Arabian society. Conservative attitudes towards gender roles and relations continue to shape the lives of both men and women, and gender segregation remains a customary practice in many public spaces. As the country continues to modernize and adapt to global trends, it is navigating the delicate balance between upholding its cultural and religious values while embracing the need for greater gender equality and women's empowerment.

Social Hierarchy

Social hierarchy plays a significant role in Saudi Arabian society and culture, with several factors contributing to an individual's social standing and status. The social hierarchy in Saudi Arabia can be understood through the following aspects:

Family and Tribal Affiliation

Family lineage and tribal affiliation are significant determinants of an individual's social standing in Saudi Arabian society. Some tribes and families hold a higher status due to their historical prominence, wealth, or connection to the ruling family. These affiliations can impact an individual's opportunities, social connections, and influence within the society.

Religious Authority

Religious scholars and leaders hold a high status in Saudi Arabian society due to the significant role of Islam in the country's culture and political system. These religious figures are often consulted on matters of Islamic law and serve as advisors to the government. The respect and reverence for religious authority are deeply rooted in Saudi Arabia's conservative religious values.

Economic Status

Wealth and economic status are also critical factors in determining an individual's social standing. Affluent families and successful business owners are highly regarded in Saudi Arabian society, and their wealth can provide them with influence and access to resources and opportunities.

Professional Status

Certain professions and occupations are considered prestigious in Saudi Arabia, such as doctors, engineers, and government officials. Individuals working in these fields often enjoy a higher social status and respect within society.

Gender and Age

Gender and age also play a role in shaping the social hierarchy in Saudi Arabia. Men typically hold higher status than women, and older individuals are often considered more knowledgeable and deserving of respect. This hierarchical structure is influenced by traditional Islamic and Arab cultural norms that emphasize the importance of age and gender in determining an individual's social position.

Expatriates and Foreign Workers

Saudi Arabia hosts a large expatriate population, including skilled professionals and manual laborers. The social standing of expatriates and foreign workers depends on a range of factors such as their nationality, occupation, and income. Skilled professionals may enjoy a higher social status, while manual laborers, primarily from South Asia and Africa, are often marginalized and face challenges in asserting their rights and social position.

6. RELIGION

The Role of Islam

Islam plays a central and pervasive role in Saudi Arabian society, culture, and politics. Saudi Arabia is the birthplace of Islam and home to its holiest sites, Mecca and Medina. The country follows a strict interpretation of Sunni Islam known as Wahhabism or Salafism, which greatly influences various aspects of daily life and governance. Here is an overview of the role of Islam in Saudi Arabia:

Theocratic Monarchy:

Saudi Arabia is an absolute monarchy, and its political system is deeply intertwined with Islamic principles. The Quran, the holy book of Islam, and the Sunnah, the traditions and practices of the Prophet Muhammad, are considered the main sources of law and governance in the country. The King of Saudi Arabia holds the title of Custodian of the Two Holy Mosques, emphasizing his role as the guardian of Islam's holiest sites and his commitment to uphold Islamic values.

Legal System:

The legal system in Saudi Arabia is based on Islamic law, or Sharia, which governs various aspects of daily life, including criminal, civil, family, and personal matters. Religious courts and judges known as Qadis interpret and apply Islamic law in the absence of a formal constitution. The religious police, known as the Committee for the Promotion of Virtue and Prevention of Vice, are responsible for enforcing Islamic moral codes and religious practices.

Religious Practices:

Islam is deeply ingrained in the daily lives of Saudi Arabians, with the five pillars of Islam – the declaration of faith, prayer, almsgiving, fasting, and pilgrimage – forming the foundation of religious practices. Muslims in Saudi Arabia are expected to pray five times a day, give a portion of their income to charity, fast during the month of Ramadan, and perform the Hajj pilgrimage to Mecca if they are financially and physically able.

Segregation of Genders:

Islamic teachings and principles greatly influence gender roles and relations in Saudi Arabia. The country has traditionally practiced strict gender segregation in public spaces, with separate areas designated for people in places like restaurants, banks, and public transportation. This segregation is also enforced in educational and professional environments, with separate institutions for people and limited interaction between the sexes.

Dress Code:

Islamic modesty codes significantly influence the dress code in Saudi Arabia, particularly for women. Women are expected to wear the abaya, a loose-fitting black cloak, and a headscarf to cover their hair in public. Some women also choose to wear the niqab, which covers the face except for the eyes. Men typically wear the thobe, a long white robe, and a head covering called the ghutra or shemagh.

Religious Education:

Religious education forms a significant part of the curriculum in Saudi Arabian schools, with students taught Islamic history, jurisprudence, and theology. Religious scholars and leaders play a crucial role in shaping the education system and ensuring that Islamic values are upheld in the teaching and learning process.

Religious Institutions

Religious institutions play a prominent role in Saudi Arabian society and culture, reflecting the crucial importance of Islam in the country. These institutions not only maintain and promote Islamic values and practices but also hold considerable influence over various aspects of daily life and governance. Here are some of the key religious institutions in Saudi Arabia:

Mosques:

Mosques serve as the primary places of worship for Muslims in Saudi Arabia. They are not only used for daily prayers but also as centers for religious education, community gatherings, and social events. The two most significant mosques in Saudi Arabia are the Masjid al-Haram in Mecca, which houses the Kaaba, and the Masjid al-Nabawi in Medina, the burial place of the Prophet Muhammad.

Ministry of Islamic Affairs, Dawah, and Guidance:

This government ministry is responsible for overseeing religious affairs in Saudi Arabia, including the administration and maintenance of mosques, the promotion of Islamic teachings, and the management of religious endowments (awqaf). The ministry also supervises Islamic propagation (dawah) activities, both domestically and internationally, and provides guidance on religious matters to the Saudi population.

Islamic Universities and Colleges:

Saudi Arabia is home to several Islamic universities and colleges that provide religious education, including the Islamic University of Madinah, Umm al-Qura University in Mecca, and Imam Muhammad ibn Saud Islamic University in Riyadh. These institutions offer various degrees in Islamic studies, including theology, jurisprudence, Quranic studies, and Islamic history. Graduates from these institutions often become religious scholars, teachers, or advisors to the government and other institutions.

The Council of Senior Scholars:

The Council of Senior Scholars is a government-appointed body of religious scholars that advises the king on matters related to Islamic law and governance. The council is responsible for issuing fatwas (religious rulings) on assorted topics, which can influence legislation and public policy. The council's opinions hold considerable weight in Saudi society, reflecting the high regard for religious authority in the country.

The Committee for the Promotion of Virtue and Prevention of Vice (CPVPV):

Also known as the religious police, the CPVPV is tasked with enforcing Islamic moral codes and religious practices in Saudi Arabia. The CPVPV has the authority to arrest and detain individuals for perceived violations of Islamic law, such as not adhering to the dress code, engaging in gender mixing, or consuming alcohol. However, recent reforms have curtailed the powers of the CPVPV, and their role in society has been diminished.

Charitable Organizations:

Numerous charitable organizations in Saudi Arabia focus on promoting Islamic values and providing social services, such as education, healthcare, and financial aid to the needy. These organizations operate under the supervision of the government and often receive funding from private donations and religious endowments.

Practices

Religious practices in Saudi Arabia are deeply rooted in Islam, as the country follows a strict interpretation of Sunni Islam known as Wahhabism or Salafism. The five pillars of Islam form the foundation of religious practices in Saudi Arabia, shaping the daily lives of the Saudi population. Here is an overview of the key religious practices in Saudi Arabia:

Prayer (Salah):

Praying five times a day is a fundamental religious practice for Muslims in Saudi Arabia. The daily prayers are performed at dawn (Fajr), noon (Dhuhr), mid-afternoon (Asr), sunset (Maghrib), and night (Isha). Muslims are required to perform ritual ablutions before prayer and face the Kaaba in Mecca while praying. Mosques broadcast the call to prayer (adhan) through loudspeakers, and businesses often close during prayer times to allow employees to participate.

Fasting (Sawm):

Fasting during the month of Ramadan is an essential religious practice for adult Muslims in Saudi Arabia, except for those who are ill, pregnant, breastfeeding, menstruating, or traveling. Fasting begins at dawn and ends at sunset, with Muslims abstaining from food, drink, and other physical needs during daylight hours. The pre-dawn meal is called suhoor, and the fast is broken with a meal called iftar after sunset.

Almsgiving (Zakat):

Zakat is a form of obligatory charity required of all eligible Muslims in Saudi Arabia. It involves giving a specific portion of one's wealth (typically 2.5% of savings and assets) to those in need, such as the poor, orphans, and travelers. Zakat is considered a way of purifying one's wealth and helping to create social equality.

Pilgrimage (Hajj):

The Hajj pilgrimage to Mecca is a mandatory religious practice for Muslims in Saudi Arabia who are financially and physically able to undertake the journey. It is one of the largest annual gatherings globally and takes place during the Islamic month of Dhu al-Hijjah. Pilgrims perform a series of rituals, including the circumambulation of the Kaaba, the standing at the plain of Arafat, and the symbolic stoning of the devil at the Jamarat in Mina.

The Umrah Pilgrimage:

Umrah is a lesser pilgrimage to Mecca that can be performed at any time of the year. While not obligatory, it is highly recommended for Muslims to perform Umrah. The rituals involved in Umrah are similar to those of the Hajj, including the circumambulation of the Kaaba and the walking between the hills of Safa and Marwah.

Religious Celebrations and Holidays:

Saudi Arabia observes several Islamic holidays, such as Eid al-Fitr, which marks the end of Ramadan, and Eid al-Adha, which coincides with the Hajj pilgrimage and commemorates Prophet Ibrahim's willingness to sacrifice his son. These holidays are marked by communal prayers, feasting, and charitable activities.

7. CUSTOMS AND ETIQUETTE

Greetings

Greetings are an essential aspect of Saudi Arabian customs and etiquette. They reflect the importance of respect, hospitality, and interpersonal relationships in Saudi culture. Here are some key points to keep in mind when greeting someone in Saudi Arabia:

Traditional Greeting

The traditional greeting among Saudis is "As-salamu alaykum," which means "peace be upon you." The appropriate response is "Wa alaykum as-salam," meaning "and upon you be peace." This greeting is common among Muslims and reflects the importance of peace and goodwill in Islamic culture.

Handshakes

When greeting someone of the same gender, a handshake is common. It is customary to shake hands with the right hand, as the left hand is considered unclean. Handshakes in Saudi Arabia can be longer than in Western cultures, and it is important not to withdraw your hand too quickly, as this may be seen as impolite.

Physical Contact

Physical contact between people of the same gender is common in Saudi Arabia. Men may engage in a close embrace or even kiss on the cheeks when greeting close friends or relatives. Women also tend to greet each other with a hug or a kiss on the cheek. However, physical contact between men and women who are not closely related is generally avoided due to cultural and religious norms.

Gender Segregation

In line with the conservative nature of Saudi society, men and women who are not related or married are generally expected to maintain a respectful distance from each other. When greeting someone of the opposite gender, it is crucial to be aware of these social norms. Avoid initiating physical contact, such as a handshake, with someone of the opposite gender unless they extend their hand first.

Addressing People

When addressing someone in Saudi Arabia, it is essential to show respect by using appropriate titles. Use the person's full name or their professional title, such as "Doctor" or "Engineer," followed by their first name. It is also common to address people using honorifics such as "Sayyid" for men or "Sayyida" for women, which means "sir" or "madam," respectively.

Age and Seniority

Age and seniority play a key role in Saudi Arabian etiquette. When entering a room or greeting a group of people, it is customary to greet the eldest or most senior person first, as a sign of respect. Be mindful of acknowledging and greeting older individuals in any social or professional setting.

Social Interactions

Social interactions in Saudi Arabia are shaped by the country's deep-rooted traditions, Islamic values, and the importance placed on hospitality and respect. Here are some key aspects of social interactions in Saudi Arabia:

Hospitality

Hospitality is a central aspect of Saudi culture, and guests are often treated with great warmth and generosity. When visiting a Saudi home, it is customary to be offered refreshments such as coffee, tea, or dates. Accepting these offerings is a sign of respect and appreciation for your host's hospitality.

Invitations

If you are invited to a Saudi home, it is important to RSVP promptly and arrive on time. Punctuality is valued, and arriving late may be considered disrespectful. When attending a social gathering, it is customary to bring a small gift, such as chocolates or flowers, as a token of appreciation for your host.

Dress Code

Saudi Arabia is a conservative society, and modest clothing is expected, particularly for women. Women should wear loose-fitting clothing that covers their arms, legs, and hair. Men should also dress modestly, wearing long pants and avoiding sleeveless shirts or shorts.

Conversation Topics

In Saudi social interactions, it is important to be mindful of the topics you discuss. Avoid sensitive subjects such as politics, religion, or personal matters, especially with acquaintances or in mixed company. Stick to neutral topics such as sports, travel, and culture to maintain a respectful and harmonious atmosphere.

Gender Segregation

Social gatherings in Saudi Arabia may be segregated by gender, particularly in more conservative circles. Be prepared to socialize with members of your own gender and respect any boundaries set by your host. It is also essential to be aware of gender norms when interacting with members of a different sex, such as avoiding physical contact and maintaining a respectful distance.

Respect for Elders

Showing respect for elders is an important aspect of Saudi etiquette. Be sure to greet older individuals first, offer them your seat if necessary, and listen attentively when they speak.

Personal Space

While Saudis may stand closer to each other than people from some Western cultures, it is still important to be mindful of personal space, particularly when interacting with the opposite gender. Maintain an appropriate distance to respect cultural norms and make others feel comfortable.

Non-Verbal Communication

Non-verbal cues play a crucial role in Saudi Arabian social interactions. Avoiding direct eye contact with members of a different sex is a sign of respect. Be aware of your body language and facial expressions, as these can convey a great deal about your intentions and emotions.

Business Etiquette

In business settings, it is essential to be punctual, professional, and respectful. Handshakes are common among men but should be initiated by the Saudi counterpart. In business meetings, always address people by their professional titles or use the honorific "Sayyid" for men and "Sayyida" for women.

Hospitality

Hospitality is a central aspect of Saudi Arabian culture and is deeply rooted in its history and Islamic values. The people of Saudi Arabia take pride in extending warmth, generosity, and kindness towards their guests. Here are some key aspects of hospitality in Saudi Arabia:

Welcoming Guests

When welcoming guests, hosts in Saudi Arabia make every effort to ensure their comfort and satisfaction. Guests are often greeted with a warm and friendly atmosphere, and hosts will engage in conversation to make them feel at ease.

Refreshments

Upon arrival, guests are usually offered refreshments such as Arabic coffee (gahwa), tea, and dates. It is customary for the host to serve the coffee, pouring it into small cups for the guests. It is polite to accept these refreshments, as it signifies your appreciation of the host's hospitality.

Meals

When invited to a Saudi home for a meal, it is essential to remember that dining etiquette is an important aspect of their hospitality. Meals are often served on a large communal platter, with guests seated on the floor or around a low table. It is common to eat with your hands, particularly when sharing a communal dish. Always use your right hand for eating, as the left hand is considered unclean. Make sure to wash your hands before and after the meal.

Gifts

When visiting a Saudi home, it is customary to bring a small gift for the host, such as chocolates, sweets, or flowers. The gift is a token of appreciation and a way to show your gratitude for their hospitality.

Dress Code

Dressing modestly and conservatively is an essential aspect of Saudi hospitality. When visiting a Saudi home, ensure that your clothing adheres to cultural norms, with women wearing loose-fitting garments that cover their arms, legs, and hair, and men wearing long pants and avoiding sleeveless shirts or shorts.

Time Spent with Guests

Saudi hosts often spend a considerable amount of time with their guests, engaging in conversation, and ensuring their comfort. It is not unusual for a visit to last several hours, as this is a way to demonstrate the host's commitment to their guest's well-being.

Saying Goodbye

When leaving a Saudi home, it is important to express your gratitude for the host's hospitality. Offer your thanks for their warmth and generosity and let them know that you enjoyed your time spent in their company.

8. COMMUNICATION

Language

Language plays a crucial role in communication in Saudi Arabia, as it reflects the nation's rich cultural heritage and Islamic identity. Arabic is the official language of Saudi Arabia and serves as the primary means of communication.

Arabic Language

Arabic, a Semitic language, is spoken by the majority of the population in Saudi Arabia. It has various dialects across the Arab world, with the Saudi Arabian dialect being part of the broader group of Peninsular Arabic dialects. The official and most commonly used form of Arabic is Modern Standard Arabic (MSA), which is used in government, media, education, and formal written communication. MSA is derived from Classical Arabic, the language of the Quran, and is understood by Arabic speakers across the region.

Local Dialects

While MSA is the standard form of Arabic used in formal settings, spoken Arabic varies from region to region in Saudi Arabia. The Hejazi dialect, for example, is spoken in the western region, including cities like Jeddah, Makkah, and Madinah. The Najdi dialect is spoken in the central region, including the capital city, Riyadh. In the eastern region, the Gulf dialect is spoken, which shares similarities with dialects spoken in other Gulf Cooperation Council (GCC) countries.

English Language

English is widely spoken as a second language in Saudi Arabia, particularly in business and educational settings. Many Saudis have a good command of English, as it is taught in schools from an early age and is the medium of instruction in many universities. Expatriates and visitors who are not fluent in Arabic will generally be able to communicate effectively in English, especially in urban centers.

Non-Arabic Languages

In addition to Arabic and English, other languages may be spoken by foreign workers and expatriates living in Saudi Arabia. Languages like Urdu, Hindi, Bengali, Tagalog, and Indonesian are spoken by individuals from countries such as India, Pakistan,

Bangladesh, the Philippines, and Indonesia, who make up a sizable portion of the workforce in the Kingdom.

Non-Verbal Cues

Non-verbal communication plays a significant role in Saudi Arabian culture, as it conveys respect, politeness, and understanding. Being aware of these non-verbal cues can help facilitate smoother interactions and avoid misunderstandings. Here are some key aspects of non-verbal communication in Saudi Arabia:

Personal Space

Saudi Arabians typically stand closer during conversations compared to Western norms. This close proximity is a sign of warmth and friendliness. It is essential to respect this cultural difference and avoid stepping back or creating more distance, as this may be perceived as cold or disinterested behavior.

Touch

Physical contact between members of the same gender is common in Saudi Arabia. It is not unusual for men to hold hands, embrace, or kiss on the cheeks as a sign of friendship and affection. However, physical contact between unrelated men and women is generally avoided due to religious and cultural reasons. Avoid initiating physical contact with someone of the opposite gender unless they do so first.

Eye Contact

Maintaining eye contact during conversations is essential, as it conveys trust and sincerity. However, staring for prolonged periods can be considered intrusive, so it is crucial to strike a balance between maintaining eye contact and occasionally looking away.

Gestures

Gestures are an integral part of communication in Saudi Arabia, with certain hand movements carrying specific meanings. For example, to indicate "no" or "stop," you can wave your hand back and forth, palm facing outwards. To signal "come here," extend your arm with the palm facing down and make a scooping motion. Be aware that pointing with your index finger can be considered impolite; instead, use your whole hand to gesture towards something.

Facial Expressions

Facial expressions can provide valuable context to the meaning behind spoken words. Smiling and maintaining a friendly demeanor is essential when interacting with others.

However, avoid excessive expressions of emotions, as Saudis may consider this inappropriate or unprofessional.

Posture

Maintaining a relaxed and respectful posture is vital in Saudi culture. When seated, avoid crossing your legs in a way that exposes the sole of your shoe to others, as this is considered disrespectful. Also, do not rest your feet on tables or chairs, as this is seen as impolite.

Business Communication

Business communication in Saudi Arabia is influenced by the country's cultural and religious values. To ensure smooth and successful business interactions, it is essential to be aware of the following aspects of business communication in Saudi Arabia:

Formality

Saudi Arabian business culture places importance on formality and politeness. Address your Saudi counterparts using their professional titles (e.g., Doctor, Engineer) or their full names. Use titles like "Mr." or "Mrs." when addressing someone whose professional title is unknown. Avoid using first names unless invited to do so.

Relationship Building

Personal relationships and trust are crucial in Saudi business culture. Expect to spend time building rapport and getting to know your Saudi counterparts before discussing business matters. Meetings may begin with small talk about family, health, or even the weather, which is an essential aspect of establishing trust.

Indirect Communication Style

Saudis tend to communicate indirectly to maintain politeness and avoid confrontation. They may use diplomatic language or express their opinions cautiously to avoid causing offense. Be attentive to non-verbal cues and subtle hints, as they may be used to convey disagreement or dissatisfaction.

Decision-Making Process

Decision-making in Saudi businesses is often centralized, with senior managers or company owners making the final decisions. Be prepared for a longer decision-making process, as it may involve multiple meetings and consultations with various stakeholders.

Patience and Flexibility

Saudi business culture values patience and flexibility. Expect delays or last-minute changes to meeting schedules, as Saudis often prioritize relationship-building and personal commitments over strict adherence to schedules. Be patient and adapt to changes when they occur.

Negotiation

In Saudi Arabia, negotiation is an expected part of the business process. Be prepared to engage in discussions about prices, terms, or conditions. Maintain a respectful and polite demeanor, even when discussing disagreements or expressing dissatisfaction.

Business Attire

Dress conservatively and professionally when attending business meetings in Saudi Arabia. Men should wear suits, while women should dress modestly, covering their arms and legs, and wear a headscarf if attending meetings with conservative clients.

Business Cards

Exchange business cards with your right hand or both hands, as the left hand is considered unclean in Arab culture. Have your business card translated into Arabic on one side to demonstrate respect for your Saudi counterparts.

9. BUSINESS CULTURE AND PRACTICES

Business Etiquette

Business etiquette in Saudi Arabia is influenced by the country's cultural and religious values. Adhering to these practices is crucial for building strong business relationships and ensuring successful interactions with Saudi counterparts. Here are some key aspects of business etiquette in Saudi Arabia:

Punctuality

While punctuality is appreciated, be aware that your Saudi counterparts may not always adhere to strict schedules. Meetings may start late or be rescheduled at the last minute due to personal or other commitments. It is essential to be patient and flexible in such situations.

Meetings

When attending a meeting, wait to be seated by your host or follow their lead. Meetings often begin with informal conversations about personal and family matters before transitioning to business discussions. This is an essential part of establishing trust and rapport.

Business Gifts

Gift-giving is not as common in Saudi business culture as in some other countries. However, if you choose to give a gift, ensure it is modest and tasteful. Gifts should not be extravagant, as this may be interpreted as a bribe. Avoid giving alcohol or items made of pigskin, as these are forbidden in Islam.

Business Dining

If invited to a business dinner, observe proper dining etiquette. Arrive on time but be prepared for a more relaxed atmosphere compared to formal business meetings. Use your right hand for eating and passing items, as the left hand is considered unclean. Follow your host's lead and wait for them to begin eating before starting yourself. Do not leave immediately after the meal, as this may be seen as impolite.

Respect for Islamic Practices

As Saudi Arabia is an Islamic country, it is essential to respect local customs and religious practices. During the holy month of Ramadan, be mindful that your Saudi counterparts may be fasting during daylight hours, and business hours may be reduced. Avoid eating, drinking, or smoking in public during this time.

Gender Segregation

In Saudi Arabia, gender segregation is common in public spaces and some workplaces. Be aware of this when planning meetings or events, and always respect local customs regarding interactions between men and women.

Conservatism

Saudi Arabian culture is conservative, and this is reflected in their business practices. Be aware of your actions and language to ensure you do not inadvertently offend your counterparts. Avoid discussing sensitive topics like politics, religion, or the royal family, as these conversations can be considered inappropriate.

Dress Code

Dress conservatively when attending business meetings in Saudi Arabia. Men should wear suits, while women should wear modest clothing that covers their arms, legs, and a headscarf if meeting with conservative clients.

Negotiations

Negotiations in Saudi Arabia are influenced by the country's cultural and religious values. Understanding the nuances of Saudi negotiation practices is essential for successful business dealings. Here are some key aspects of negotiations in Saudi Arabian business culture:

Relationship Building

Establishing trust and rapport is critical before engaging in negotiations. Saudi business culture places significant importance on personal relationships, so expect to invest time in getting to know your counterparts before discussing business matters.

Patience and Persistence

Negotiations can be lengthy and may require several meetings to reach a final agreement. Patience is highly valued in Saudi culture, so avoid rushing the negotiation process or applying undue pressure on your counterparts.

Indirect Communication

Saudis tend to use an indirect communication style to maintain politeness and avoid confrontation. They may express their opinions cautiously or use diplomatic language to avoid causing offense. Be attentive to non-verbal cues and subtle hints, as they may be used to convey disagreement or dissatisfaction.

Consensus Building

Decision-making in Saudi businesses is often hierarchical, with senior managers or company owners making the final decisions. However, obtaining consensus among various stakeholders is also essential. Be prepared to present your proposals to different individuals or departments and allow time for deliberation and consultation.

Saving Face

Avoid putting your Saudi counterparts in a position where they may lose face or be embarrassed in front of others. If disagreements arise, address them privately and diplomatically to maintain harmony and respect.

Bargaining

Bargaining is a common aspect of negotiations in Saudi Arabia. Be prepared to engage in discussions about prices, terms, or conditions. Maintain a respectful and polite demeanor, even when expressing dissatisfaction or disagreements.

Flexibility

Be open to making concessions and adjusting your expectations to reach a mutually beneficial agreement. Demonstrating flexibility and a willingness to compromise can help foster goodwill and strengthen business relationships.

Contracts and Agreements

Once an agreement is reached, contracts should be detailed and explicit, outlining the responsibilities of all parties involved. However, be aware that Saudi counterparts may view contracts as a starting point for further negotiations rather than a binding document. Building trust and maintaining open communication is crucial for ensuring successful long-term partnerships.

Workplace Expectations

Workplace expectations in Saudi Arabia are influenced by the country's cultural and religious values. Understanding these expectations is essential for navigating the professional environment and fostering strong working relationships. Here are some key aspects of workplace expectations in Saudi Arabian business culture:

Hierarchy and Respect

Saudi workplaces are often hierarchical, with a clear distinction between management and employees. Show respect to senior managers and decision-makers, addressing them by their formal titles and seeking their input when necessary. It is essential to demonstrate respect for elders and those in authority in the Saudi working environment.

Gender Segregation

Gender segregation is still prevalent in many Saudi workplaces, particularly in more conservative organizations. Be aware of this when interacting with colleagues and clients of the opposite sex. Maintain a respectful and professional demeanor and avoid any behaviors that could be perceived as inappropriate or overly familiar.

Work Hours and Prayer Times

Work hours in Saudi Arabia may differ from those in Western countries, with many businesses operating on a split schedule to accommodate daily prayers. Be prepared to adapt to local working hours and show respect for your colleagues' religious obligations by not scheduling meetings or events during prayer times.

Dress Code

Conservative attire is expected in Saudi workplaces. Men should wear suits or traditional attire, while women should dress modestly, covering their arms, legs, and hair if working in a conservative environment. It is essential to maintain a professional appearance to show respect for local customs and cultural expectations.

Communication Style

Saudi business culture values indirect communication to avoid confrontation and maintain politeness. Be mindful of this when expressing your opinions or providing feedback. Use diplomatic language and avoid blunt statements that could cause offense or tension.

Teamwork and Collaboration

Saudi workplaces often value teamwork and collaboration, with employees expected to contribute to the success of the team and support their colleagues. Demonstrate your willingness to collaborate by offering assistance, sharing knowledge, and participating in group projects or initiatives.

Performance and Recognition

Hard work and dedication are appreciated in Saudi workplaces, but public displays of recognition or praise may be uncommon. Instead, feedback may be provided privately or through subtle gestures. It is essential to remain humble and avoid boasting about your achievements or successes.

Adaptability

Saudi Arabia is undergoing significant economic and social changes, and being adaptable and open to new ideas is increasingly important in the workplace. Show your willingness to learn and adapt to new processes, technologies, or ways of working to demonstrate your commitment to your role and the organization.

10. DRESS CODE AND APPEARANCE

Traditional Clothing

In Saudi Arabia, traditional clothing plays a significant role in the country's culture and identity. Both men and women wear specific attire that adheres to the conservative values of the society. Here is an overview of traditional clothing in Saudi Arabia:

Men's Clothing:

Thobe: The Thobe (or thawb) is a long, ankle-length garment, usually made of light fabrics like cotton or linen, which is worn by Saudi men. It is designed to be loose-fitting and comfortable, particularly in the hot desert climate. Thobes are typically white but can also be found in other colors like beige, gray, or blue, particularly during the winter months.

Shemagh: The Shemagh (or ghutra) is a large, square-shaped cloth that is worn as a head covering. It is folded into a triangle and secured onto the head with a black or white circlet called an "agal." The shemagh is typically worn in red and white or plain white patterns, although other colors may be used for specific occasions or personal preference.

Bisht: The Bisht is a formal cloak worn by men over their thobe during special occasions, such as weddings or official events. It is typically made of a heavier fabric like wool or camel hair and features intricate embroidery along the edges. The bisht is often worn by high-ranking officials or members of the royal family.

Women's Clothing:

Abaya: The Abaya is a loose, full-length cloak worn by Saudi women to cover their clothing when in public. It is typically black and made of lightweight fabrics, like crepe or chiffon, to ensure comfort in the hot climate. Abayas can range from simple designs to those with intricate embellishments or patterns.

Hijab: The Hijab is a headscarf worn by many Saudi women to cover their hair in public, as a symbol of modesty and religious observance. Hijabs come in various styles, colors, and fabrics, allowing women to express their personal preferences while adhering to cultural norms.

Niqab: Some Saudi women choose to wear a niqab, which is a veil that covers the face, leaving only the eyes visible. The niqab is often worn in addition to the hijab and is considered a more conservative form of covering.

Dress Standards

In Saudi Arabia, adhering to conservative dress standards is crucial, as it reflects the country's cultural values and religious beliefs. Both locals and foreigners are expected to dress modestly and respectfully in public spaces. Here is an overview of the dress standards in Saudi Arabia:

Men's Dress Standards:

- Men should wear long pants and a collared shirt, preferably with long sleeves. Short sleeves are acceptable in less formal settings, but sleeveless shirts or tank tops should be avoided.
- While Western-style clothing is generally acceptable, particularly in cities and business environments, attire should remain modest and conservative.
- Shorts are generally considered inappropriate in public, except in private settings like the beach or a swimming pool.
- Clothes should be clean and well-maintained, as appearances matter in Saudi society.

Women's Dress Standards:

- Women are expected to wear loose-fitting, modest clothing that covers their arms and legs. Clothing should not be tight, revealing, or transparent.
- In public spaces or when in the presence of unrelated men, women should wear a headscarf to cover their hair. Wearing an abaya, a full-length cloak, is also common for both Saudi and non-Saudi women.
- While wearing a niqab (face veil) is not mandatory for non-Saudi women, some may choose to wear it to show respect for local customs or in more conservative areas.
- Western-style clothing is acceptable underneath an abaya but should still adhere to modesty standards.

Business Dress Standards:

- In the business environment, men should wear suits or formal attire, with a tie and dress shoes. Traditional clothing like a thobe and shemagh is also acceptable, particularly for Saudi men.
- Women should dress conservatively in professional settings, wearing a suit or a dress with a jacket, ensuring their attire covers their arms and legs. A headscarf should be worn in business settings, and an abaya may be necessary, depending on the organization's culture.

Special Considerations:

- When visiting religious sites, such as mosques, both men and women should dress conservatively and adhere to strict modesty standards. Women should cover their hair with a headscarf, and it is recommended to wear an abaya as well.
- During social gatherings or events, it is essential to observe the dress code specified by the host or the venue, which may include wearing traditional attire or adhering to specific dress standards.

11. FOOD AND CULINARY TRADITIONS

Typical Dishes

Saudi Arabian cuisine is a delightful mix of flavors, spices, and textures that reflect the country's rich cultural heritage. Traditional Saudi Arabian dishes are typically made with locally sourced ingredients such as rice, meat, vegetables, and a variety of spices. Here are some of the most popular and delicious dishes to try in Saudi Arabia:

- Kabsa: Kabsa is a famous Saudi Arabian dish made of long-grain rice, meat (usually chicken, lamb, or goat), and a mix of spices such as black lime, bay leaves, and cardamom. The dish is often garnished with fried onions, raisins, and almonds, giving it a unique blend of savory and sweet flavors.
- Mandi: Similar to Kabsa, Mandi is a traditional rice dish made with slow-cooked meat (usually chicken or lamb) and a mixture of spices. The meat is cooked in a tandoor (an underground clay oven), which gives it a distinct smoky flavor. The dish is often served with a side of yogurt or a simple tomato-based sauce.
- Shawarma: Shawarma is a popular Middle Eastern dish that has become a staple in Saudi Arabia. It consists of marinated meat (usually chicken or lamb) that is grilled on a vertical spit and then thinly sliced. The meat is typically served in a wrap or a flatbread with vegetables, pickles, and a variety of sauces.
- Mutabbaq: This savory stuffed pancake is a popular street food in Saudi Arabia. Mutabbaq is made with a thin dough filled with a mixture of eggs, minced meat, onions, and various spices, then folded and fried until golden brown. It is usually served with a side of yogurt or a spicy tomato-based sauce.
- Samboosa: Also known as samosa, samboosa is a popular appetizer or snack in Saudi Arabia. These small, triangular pastries are filled with a variety of ingredients such as minced meat, vegetables, or cheese, and are deep-fried to achieve a crispy texture.
- Falafel: A popular Middle Eastern dish, falafel consists of deep-fried balls or patties made from ground chickpeas or fava beans, mixed with a variety of spices and herbs. Falafel is often served with tahini sauce, pickles, and fresh vegetables, either in a wrap or as part of a mezze platter.
- Jareesh: A traditional Saudi Arabian dish, Jareesh is a porridge-like dish made from crushed wheat, meat (usually chicken or lamb), onions, and a blend of spices. It is typically served with a side of yogurt or laban (a type of fermented milk).

- Umm Ali: This delicious dessert is similar to bread pudding, made with layers of puff pastry, milk, sugar, and various nuts and raisins. Umm Ali is often flavored with rose water or orange blossom water and served warm, topped with whipped cream or a scoop of ice cream.
- Dates and Arabic Coffee: No meal in Saudi Arabia is complete without serving dates and Arabic coffee. The coffee is made from lightly roasted coffee beans, cardamom, and sometimes saffron, and is typically served with fresh dates as a gesture of hospitality.

Dining Etiquette

Dining etiquette in Saudi Arabia reflects the country's cultural values and traditions, with an emphasis on hospitality, respect, and social connections. When dining with Saudi Arabians, it is essential to be aware of these customs and practices to ensure a positive and respectful experience.

- Hand Washing: Before and after the meal, it is customary to wash your hands. In traditional settings, a handwashing basin may be brought to the table for guests to use.
- Seating Arrangements: In Saudi Arabia, guests are typically seated according to their age, social status, or professional rank. The most senior or honored guest is usually offered the best seat at the table.
- Eating with Hands: In traditional Saudi Arabian settings, it is common to eat with your hands, specifically the right hand, as the left hand is considered unclean. If utensils are provided, it is acceptable to use them. However, it is essential to avoid using your left hand for eating or passing dishes.
- Communal Plates: In many Saudi Arabian households, food is served on communal plates from which everyone eats. It is polite to eat from the section of the plate closest to you and avoid reaching across the plate.
- Serving Food: When dishes are being served, it is customary for the host to serve the guests, starting with the most senior or honored guest. It is considered impolite to refuse food when it is offered to you.
- Taking Small Portions: It is polite to take small portions of food at a time and accept second helpings if offered. This shows appreciation and enjoyment of the meal.
- Eating Slowly: Eating slowly and engaging in conversation is a sign of respect and appreciation for the meal and the company. It is considered impolite to eat quickly or in silence.

- Expressing Gratitude: It is essential to thank the host for the meal, both during and after the meal. Complementing the food and the host's hospitality is a sign of appreciation and respect.
- Leaving Food on the Plate: In Saudi Arabia, it is customary to leave a small amount of food on your plate at the end of the meal. This gesture signifies that you are full and that the host has provided you with enough food.
- Tea and Coffee: After the meal, tea or Arabic coffee is usually served as a sign of hospitality. It is polite to accept at least one cup.

Social Aspects of Eating

In Saudi Arabian culture, food plays a significant role in fostering social bonds, building relationships, and strengthening community ties. The social aspects of eating in Saudi Arabia are deeply rooted in the values of hospitality, generosity, and respect, which are evident in various aspects of dining and sharing meals.

- Hospitality: Saudi Arabian culture is known for its warm and welcoming hospitality. Inviting people to share a meal, whether in a home or at a restaurant, is a common way to strengthen relationships and build connections. It is customary for hosts to provide an abundance of food to demonstrate their generosity and care for their guests.
- Family gatherings: Meals are often a time for families to come together and share in each other's company. In Saudi Arabia, families are close-knit, and mealtimes serve as an opportunity for family members to catch up on each other's lives, discuss important issues, and maintain strong bonds.
- Religious celebrations: Food plays a central role in many religious celebrations and observances in Saudi Arabia. During the Islamic holy month of Ramadan, families and friends gather to break their fast together with a meal called iftar. Similarly, the feast of Eid al-Fitr, which marks the end of Ramadan, and Eid al-Adha, the feast of sacrifice, are both marked by large gatherings and the sharing of meals.
- Social etiquette: Dining in Saudi Arabia comes with its own set of social etiquette and customs that are important to observe. For example, it is considered polite to accept an invitation to a meal and to arrive on time or slightly later than the specified time. During the meal, engaging in conversation and showing appreciation for the food are signs of respect and consideration for the host.
- Sharing food: In many Saudi households, it is common for food to be served on large communal plates or platters, with everyone eating together. This practice emphasizes the importance of sharing and togetherness in Saudi culture.

- Gift-giving: When invited to someone's home for a meal, it is customary to bring a small gift as a token of appreciation. Common gifts include sweets, chocolates, or flowers.
- Business and social gatherings: In Saudi Arabia, business relationships are often strengthened through social interactions that involve sharing meals. Inviting business partners or colleagues to a meal can help build trust and create a more personal connection.

12. EDUCATION SYSTEM AND VALUES

Structure

Saudi Arabia's education system is designed to promote the values of the nation, with a strong emphasis on Islamic teachings, cultural identity, and patriotism. The education system is overseen by the Ministry of Education and is structured in a way that provides access to education for all citizens, from early childhood to higher education. Here is an overview of the structure of the education system in Saudi Arabia:

- Pre-primary Education: Pre-primary education, also known as kindergarten, is available for children aged 3 to 5 years old. Although not compulsory, this stage aims to prepare children for primary school and introduces them to basic educational concepts, social skills, and Islamic teachings.
- Primary Education: Primary education is compulsory and free for all Saudi Arabian children aged 6 to 12. This stage consists of six years of schooling, where students learn basic subjects such as Arabic, Islamic studies, mathematics, science, and social studies, with a strong focus on religious and moral education.
- Intermediate Education: Following primary education, students attend intermediate school for three years, usually from ages 12 to 15. This stage continues to build on the subjects taught in primary school and introduces additional subjects, such as English, computer studies, and physical education.
- Secondary Education: Secondary education is the final stage of compulsory schooling, lasting for three years and typically attended by students aged 15 to 18. At this stage, students can choose between two tracks: general secondary education or vocational secondary education. General secondary education is further divided into three streams: scientific, administrative, and Islamic studies. Vocational secondary education focuses on preparing students for specific trades and industries.
- Higher Education: After completing secondary education, students can choose to pursue higher education at universities, colleges, or technical institutes. Saudi Arabia has numerous public and private universities, which offer undergraduate and postgraduate degrees in various fields. Admission to universities is competitive, with entrance exams and high school grades determining eligibility.
- Adult and Continuing Education: Saudi Arabia recognizes the importance of lifelong learning and provides opportunities for adults to continue their education through various programs, such as vocational training centers, literacy programs, and distance learning courses.

Access

Access to education is a high priority in Saudi Arabia, as the country recognizes the importance of an educated population for its development and progress. Over the past few decades, Saudi Arabia has made significant investments in expanding and improving its education system, resulting in increased access to education for its citizens.

- Gender Access: Historically, education in Saudi Arabia was mainly focused on males, with limited opportunities for females. However, significant strides have been made to promote gender equality in education. Today, females have access to all levels of education, from primary to higher education, and female enrollment rates have increased dramatically. This has been facilitated by the establishment of girls' schools and the expansion of women's colleges and universities.
- Rural Access: The government has focused on expanding access to education in rural areas by building schools, providing transportation, and offering incentives for teachers to work in remote locations. These efforts have helped to reduce disparities in access to education between urban and rural areas.
- Special Needs Access: Saudi Arabia has also taken steps to improve access to education for students with special needs. Special education programs and schools have been established to cater to students with disabilities, and mainstream schools are increasingly incorporating inclusive practices to accommodate students with diverse learning needs.
- Financial Access: Education is provided free of charge for Saudi citizens at all levels, from primary to higher education. This ensures that financial barriers do not prevent students from accessing education. Additionally, the government offers scholarships and financial aid for students pursuing higher education, both domestically and abroad.
- Technological Access: The government has invested in technology and digital resources to improve access to education and enhance the quality of teaching and learning. Initiatives such as e-learning platforms, digital libraries, and computer labs in schools have expanded access to educational resources for students and teachers alike.
- Adult Education: Adult and continuing education programs are available for Saudi citizens who wish to further their education or acquire new skills. These programs include vocational training, literacy courses, and distance learning options, providing flexible opportunities for adults to access education.

The Role of Religion in Education

In Saudi Arabia, the role of religion in education is significant, as the country is an Islamic state and adheres to a conservative interpretation of Sunni Islam, known as Wahhabism. The Saudi Arabian education system is designed to incorporate Islamic teachings and values throughout all levels of education, with a strong emphasis on promoting religious and moral education.

- Curriculum: The Saudi Arabian education curriculum is deeply rooted in Islamic teachings. Subjects like Arabic, Islamic studies, and Quranic studies form an integral part of the curriculum at all levels of education, from primary to higher education. These subjects aim to instill Islamic knowledge, values, and morals in students and to promote a strong sense of religious and national identity.
- Religious Institutions: Religious institutions play an important role in the Saudi Arabian education system. Institutions such as Islamic universities, colleges, and religious schools focus on providing Islamic education and training future religious leaders, teachers, and scholars. Additionally, mosques often provide Quranic and Islamic studies classes for children and adults alike.
- Separation of Genders: In line with the conservative Islamic values, the Saudi Arabian education system maintains strict gender segregation. Boys and girls attend separate schools and universities, with separate campuses, classrooms, and facilities. This segregation is based on the religious belief in maintaining modesty and limiting interactions between unrelated men and women.
- Teachers and School Environment: Teachers in Saudi Arabia are expected to promote Islamic values and adhere to religious guidelines in their teaching practices and personal conduct. Schools are also expected to create an environment that supports religious values, with daily prayers, observance of Islamic holidays, and the promotion of modest dress codes.
- Moral Education: In addition to academic subjects, Saudi Arabian schools focus on moral education based on Islamic principles. Students are taught values such as respect, honesty, kindness, and responsibility, with an emphasis on developing good character and strong moral behavior in line with Islamic teachings.

13. MEDIA AND POPULAR CULTURE

Newspapers

Newspapers play an essential role in the media landscape of Saudi Arabia, providing news, information, and analysis to the public. Saudi newspapers, like other forms of media in the country, are regulated by the government and are subject to censorship. Despite these limitations, newspapers continue to be a significant source of information and cultural expression for the Saudi population.

- National Newspapers: Saudi Arabia has several daily national newspapers, published in both Arabic and English. Some of the leading Arabic newspapers include Al-Riyadh, Al-Jazirah, and Al-Madina, while leading English newspapers include Arab News, Saudi Gazette, and Riyadh Daily. These newspapers cover a wide range of topics, such as politics, economy, society, and culture, while also providing international news and analysis.
- Regional Newspapers: In addition to national newspapers, Saudi Arabia also has several regional newspapers that focus on local news, events, and issues. These regional newspapers cater to the specific interests and needs of their respective communities and help to provide a more localized perspective on news and current affairs.
- Government Ownership and Control: The majority of newspapers in Saudi Arabia are either owned by the government or have close ties to the government. This means that the content of newspapers is subject to censorship and editorial control by the state. While some newspapers may present differing viewpoints, criticism of the government or the royal family is generally not tolerated.
- Online Presence: With the rise of the internet and digital media, Saudi newspapers have increasingly moved online, with many offering digital editions and news websites. This has allowed newspapers to reach a wider audience, both within Saudi Arabia and internationally. Social media platforms, such as Twitter and Facebook, have also become essential tools for newspapers to disseminate news and engage with readers.
- Challenges and Opportunities: Newspapers in Saudi Arabia face several challenges, including censorship, declining print circulation, and the rise of digital media. However, they also have the opportunity to adapt and innovate in response to these challenges. By embracing digital platforms, focusing on quality journalism, and engaging with their audience, Saudi newspapers can continue to play a vital role in the country's media landscape.

Television

Television is a popular medium for entertainment, news, and cultural expression in Saudi Arabia. The TV landscape has undergone significant changes over the years, with the introduction of satellite and digital broadcasting, as well as the rise of streaming services. Although the government heavily regulates TV content, the industry has continued to expand and diversify, offering a mix of local and international programming to Saudi viewers.

- State-Run Television: The Saudi Broadcasting Authority (SBA) is the government agency responsible for overseeing the country's television industry. SBA operates several state-run TV channels, including Saudi TV1, Saudi TV2, and Al Ekhbariya. These channels provide a mix of news, educational programming, religious content, and entertainment, reflecting the government's perspective on various issues.
- Satellite Television: The introduction of satellite TV in the 1990s significantly impacted the Saudi television landscape, providing viewers with access to a wide range of international channels. Popular satellite TV providers include Arabsat and Nilesat, which offer a mix of news, entertainment, sports, and religious programming from across the Arab world and beyond. Satellite TV has allowed Saudi viewers to access diverse perspectives and content, including Western TV shows and movies, albeit often censored or edited for local sensibilities.
- Private Channels: In addition to state-run and satellite TV channels, Saudi Arabia also has several privately-owned television channels. These channels, such as MBC Group and Rotana, offer a variety of programming, including news, entertainment, and cultural content. While these channels are subject to government regulation and censorship, they often provide a more diverse range of programming compared to state-run channels.
- Streaming Services: The rise of streaming services, such as Netflix and regional platforms like Shahid and STARZPLAY, has further diversified the TV landscape in Saudi Arabia. These services have gained popularity by offering a wide range of on-demand content, including international movies, TV series, and documentaries. The availability of streaming services has also given Saudi viewers more control over their viewing habits, allowing them to watch content at their convenience.
- Censorship and Content Regulation: The Saudi government closely monitors and censors television content to ensure it aligns with the country's cultural and religious values. This includes censoring or banning content deemed inappropriate, such as explicit scenes or criticism of the government or Islam.

Despite these restrictions, television remains an essential medium for news, entertainment, and cultural expression in Saudi Arabia.

Social Media in Saudi Society

Social media has become an essential aspect of everyday life in Saudi Arabia, with a high percentage of the population actively using various platforms. Saudi Arabia has one of the highest social media penetration rates in the Middle East, with popular platforms like Twitter, Snapchat, Instagram, and YouTube attracting millions of users. Social media has significantly impacted Saudi society, offering new avenues for communication, self-expression, and access to information while also posing challenges related to privacy and cultural values.

- Communication and Connectivity: Social media platforms have enabled Saudis to connect with friends, family, and colleagues, both within the country and abroad. The ease of communication and information sharing has facilitated the growth of online communities centered around shared interests, professional networking, and support groups.
- Self-Expression and Creativity: Social media has provided a platform for Saudis to display their talents, opinions, and creativity. From fashion influencers to political commentators, many individuals have leveraged social media to gain a following and share their perspectives on various issues. Additionally, social media platforms have allowed budding artists, musicians, and filmmakers to highlight their work and reach a wider audience.
- Access to Information: Social media has become a critical source of news and information for many Saudis, who use platforms like Twitter and Facebook to stay updated on local and global events. The accessibility of social media has also facilitated the rapid spread of information, both accurate and inaccurate, which has posed challenges related to misinformation and the need for digital literacy.
- Cultural Shifts and Youth Empowerment: The widespread use of social media has contributed to shifting cultural norms and attitudes in Saudi Arabia, particularly among younger generations. Social media has provided a space for open discussion on social, political, and religious issues, fostering greater awareness and understanding of different viewpoints. This has, in turn, contributed to a more open and inclusive society, albeit with ongoing debates and tensions surrounding traditional values and modernity.
- Privacy and Cultural Values: While social media offers numerous benefits, it has also raised concerns about privacy and the erosion of cultural values. Many Saudis are cautious about sharing personal information online, and the government closely monitors online activities to ensure adherence to local laws

and cultural norms. Additionally, the potential for social media to expose individuals to content that may not align with traditional Saudi values has led to ongoing debates about the role of social media in society.

14. ARTS, LITERATURE AND MUSIC

Saudi Arabia has a rich and diverse cultural heritage that encompasses traditional and contemporary expressions in the arts, literature, and music. These forms of cultural expression have been influenced by the country's history, religion, and regional traditions, resulting in a unique blend of artistic creativity.

Traditional Arts: Traditional Saudi Arabian art forms include calligraphy, geometric and arabesque designs, and decorative arts, such as metalwork, pottery, and textiles. These art forms often feature Islamic motifs and themes, reflecting the importance of religion in Saudi culture. Traditional handicrafts, such as weaving and embroidery, are also significant forms of artistic expression in Saudi Arabia.

Literature: Saudi Arabian literature has a rich history that dates back to pre-Islamic poetry and storytelling traditions. Classical Arabic poetry and prose, as well as Islamic texts, have been essential components of the literary landscape. In recent years, Saudi literature has become increasingly diverse, with contemporary authors exploring themes such as identity, social issues, and modern life. Notable Saudi writers include Ghazi Al-Gosaibi, Turki Al-Hamad, and Rajaa Alsanea.

Music: Traditional Saudi Arabian music is characterized by a combination of vocal and instrumental performances, often accompanied by poetry recitations. Regional musical styles, such as Hijazi, Najdi, and Southern music, display the diversity of the country's musical traditions. Traditional instruments, like the oud, qanun, and daff, play an essential role in Saudi music.

Contemporary Arts: In recent years, Saudi Arabia has witnessed a growing interest in contemporary art, with artists exploring various forms, such as painting, sculpture, photography, and digital media. These artists often address social and political issues, pushing boundaries and fostering dialogue about contemporary Saudi society. Art exhibitions, galleries, and events, such as the Jeddah Art Week, have become important platforms for highlighting and promoting contemporary Saudi art.

Film and Theatre: The Saudi film and theatre scene has experienced a resurgence in recent years, with a new generation of filmmakers, actors, and playwrights emerging. This has been facilitated by the lifting of the ban on cinemas in 2018 and the establishment of institutions such as the Saudi Film Council. Saudi films, such as "Wadjda" by Haifaa Al-Mansour and "The Perfect Candidate" by Mahmoud Sabbagh, have gained international recognition and acclaim.

Popular Culture and Media: Saudi Arabia has a thriving popular culture, with television, radio, print, and digital media playing an essential role in disseminating information and entertainment. Social media platforms have become particularly influential, providing a space for cultural expression, creativity, and the sharing of ideas among the Saudi population.

15. HOLIDAYS, FESTIVALS AND CELEBRATIONS

In Saudi Arabia, holidays, festivals, and celebrations are deeply rooted in Islamic traditions and the country's cultural heritage. The following is an overview of the major religious and national observances in Saudi Arabia:

Ramadan: Ramadan is the holiest month in the Islamic calendar, observed by Muslims worldwide as a month of fasting, prayer, reflection, and community. During Ramadan, Muslims fast from sunrise to sunset, abstaining from food, drink, and other physical needs. The pre-dawn meal is called suhoor, and the meal to break the fast at sunset is called iftar. Ramadan culminates in the festival of Eid al-Fitr.

Eid al-Fitr: This three-day festival marks the end of Ramadan and is one of the most significant religious celebrations in Saudi Arabia. Families come together to share meals, exchange gifts, and attend special prayers at mosques. It is a time for charity, forgiveness, and joyous gatherings with friends and relatives.

Eid al-Adha: Also known as the Feast of Sacrifice, Eid al-Adha is another important Islamic festival that commemorates the willingness of Ibrahim (Abraham) to sacrifice his son as an act of obedience to God. The festival lasts for three days and involves the ritual sacrifice of an animal, usually a sheep or a goat, with a portion of the meat distributed to the poor. Families and friends gather for feasts, prayers, and the exchange of gifts.

Hajj: The Hajj is the annual Islamic pilgrimage to Mecca, which is one of the Five Pillars of Islam and a religious duty that must be conducted at least once in a lifetime by all able-bodied Muslims who can afford to do so. The pilgrimage takes place during the Islamic month of Dhu al-Hijjah and involves various rituals, including the Tawaf (circumambulating the Kaaba), the Sa'i (walking between the hills of Safa and Marwah), and the symbolic stoning of the devil.

Saudi National Day: Celebrated on September 23rd each year, Saudi National Day commemorates the founding of the Kingdom of Saudi Arabia by King Abdulaziz Al Saud in 1932. The day is marked by various events and activities, including parades, fireworks, cultural performances, and patriotic songs. It is a time for the people of Saudi Arabia to express their national pride and appreciation for their country's heritage and achievements.

Al-Janadriyah Festival: This annual cultural and heritage festival takes place near Riyadh and lasts for about two weeks. It displays traditional arts, crafts, dance, music, and poetry from different regions of Saudi Arabia, offering a glimpse into the country's rich cultural heritage. The festival also features camel races, traditional sports, and exhibitions.

16. GENDER DYNAMICS AND THE STATUS OF WOMEN

Legal Rights

The status of women in Saudi Arabia has evolved significantly over the past few years, with various legal reforms and initiatives aimed at improving gender equality and women's rights. Despite these positive changes, there are still some cultural and legal restrictions that impact women's rights in the country.

Guardianship System: One of the most significant reforms in recent years has been the dismantling of the male guardianship system. Historically, this system required women to obtain permission from a male guardian (usually a father, husband, or brother) for many aspects of their lives, such as traveling, working, marrying, or even seeking medical treatment. In 2019, the Saudi government introduced reforms that allowed women to obtain passports, travel without a male guardian's permission, and register births, marriages, and divorces independently.

Right to Drive: In June 2018, Saudi Arabia lifted the ban on women driving, granting women the right to apply for a driver's license and drive without the need for a male guardian's permission. This significant change has provided women with increased mobility and independence, opening up new opportunities for education and employment.

Women in the Workforce: The Saudi Vision 2030 plan, which aims to diversify the economy and reduce its dependence on oil, has emphasized the importance of increasing women's participation in the workforce. In recent years, the government has introduced reforms to create a more inclusive work environment, including anti-discrimination and anti-harassment laws, as well as policies that mandate equal pay for equal work.

Political Participation: Women's political participation has also seen progress in Saudi Arabia. In 2015, women were granted the right to vote and run for office in municipal elections, with several women winning seats on local councils. Additionally, women have been appointed to high-ranking government positions, including ambassadorships and ministerial roles.

Family Law: In the realm of family law, women in Saudi Arabia still face some challenges. For instance, while women can now independently register marriages and divorces, they continue to face difficulties in child custody disputes and divorce proceedings. The legal age for marriage remains an issue as well, with no minimum age set for girls to marry, which can lead to child marriages.

Social Expectations

In Saudi Arabia, social expectations for women have been traditionally influenced by conservative interpretations of Islam and cultural norms. While recent reforms have improved women's rights and increased their participation in public life, social expectations continue to shape their roles and responsibilities in society.

Family and Marriage: Women in Saudi Arabia are traditionally expected to prioritize their roles as wives, mothers, and caregivers. Marriages are often arranged, and women are expected to marry within their social and economic class. Although women now have more legal autonomy in registering marriages and divorces, social expectations still play a significant role in shaping their choices within the family unit.

Modesty and Dress: Women in Saudi Arabia are expected to adhere to a strict dress code, wearing an abaya (a long, loose-fitting cloak) and a hijab (a headscarf) to cover their hair. The dress code aims to promote modesty and is enforced by religious police. However, in recent years, there has been a growing trend of women adopting more contemporary and colourful styles of abayas, reflecting a gradual shift in social attitudes.

Segregation: Gender segregation in public spaces has been a longstanding aspect of Saudi society, with designated areas for men and women in places such as restaurants, schools, and workplaces. However, recent reforms have seen a relaxation of these strict segregation policies, with more public spaces becoming gender-integrated, including entertainment venues and sports stadiums.

Education and Employment: As more women enter the workforce and pursue higher education, social expectations are gradually shifting to accommodate these changes. Women now make up a significant portion of university graduates in Saudi Arabia, and the government's Vision 2030 plan actively encourages women's participation in the workforce. However, women still face challenges in balancing their traditional roles within the family with their professional aspirations, and there may be societal resistance to women working in certain professions.

Public Conduct: Women are expected to behave modestly and conservatively in public, avoiding displays of affection or interaction with unrelated men. However, as more women enter the workforce and public life, interactions between men and women are becoming more common, leading to a gradual shift in societal expectations.

Ongoing Reforms

In recent years, Saudi Arabia has been undergoing significant reforms to improve the status of women and promote gender equality. These reforms, spearheaded by Crown Prince Mohammed bin Salman, are part of the country's ambitious Vision 2030 plan to modernize the economy and society. Some notable ongoing reforms related to gender dynamics and the status of women include:

Lifting the Driving Ban: In June 2018, the long-standing ban on women driving in Saudi Arabia was lifted. This historic move granted women greater mobility and independence, allowing them to access education, employment, and healthcare more easily.

Guardianship System Reforms: The male guardianship system has been a significant obstacle to women's autonomy in Saudi Arabia. However, recent reforms have reduced the scope of this system. For example, women no longer require a male guardian's permission to obtain a passport, travel abroad, or register a marriage or divorce. Furthermore, women can now be the legal guardians of their children, a right previously reserved for men.

Greater Participation in the Workforce: The government has set a target to increase women's participation in the workforce from 22% to 30% by 2030. New labour laws now protect women from discrimination in the workplace and mandate equal pay for equal work. Women are also increasingly entering traditionally male-dominated fields, such as engineering and aviation.

Increased Political Representation: Women's political representation has been steadily increasing, with 30 women appointed to the Shura Council in 2013. The Council, an advisory body to the King, now has a 20% female representation. Additionally, women were granted the right to vote and run in municipal elections in 2015.

Entertainment and Sports: As part of the Vision 2030 plan, the Saudi government has been investing in the entertainment sector and promoting sports for both men and women. Women can now attend public sporting events in stadiums, and the country hosted its first women's marathon in 2018.

Education and Scholarships: Women's access to education has been a significant focus of the ongoing reforms. Female students now represent over half of university graduates in Saudi Arabia, and the government offers scholarships to women for studying abroad in various fields, encouraging them to pursue higher education and professional careers.

17. TIPS FOR TRAVELLERS AND EXPATS

Safety

Saudi Arabia is generally considered a safe country for travellers and expats, but it is essential to be aware of certain safety tips to ensure a smooth and enjoyable experience. Here are some tips to keep in mind:

Follow local laws and customs: Familiarize yourself with Saudi Arabia's laws and cultural norms to avoid inadvertently breaking any rules or causing offense. This includes dressing modestly, respecting religious practices, and adhering to gender segregation rules in public spaces.

Stay updated on travel advisories: Keep an eye on travel advisories issued by your home country's government, which will provide information on any potential risks or security concerns. These advisories may be updated regularly, so it's important to stay informed.

Carry identification: Always carry your identification documents, such as your passport or iqama (residence permit), when out in public. You may be asked to present these documents at checkpoints or during random police checks.

Be cautious in public: Exercise caution in crowded places and avoid drawing unnecessary attention to yourself. It's best to keep a low profile and blend in with the local culture as much as possible.

Avoid discussing sensitive topics: Refrain from discussing sensitive political, religious, or social issues, particularly with strangers. These conversations could lead to misunderstandings or even legal trouble.

Register with your embassy: If you are an expat living in Saudi Arabia, it's a good idea to register with your home country's embassy or consulate. This will help them assist you in case of an emergency or if you require any support during your stay.

Be prepared for emergencies: Know the local emergency phone numbers and the location of the nearest hospital and embassy or consulate. Ensure you have a basic understanding of local customs and etiquette in case of an emergency.

Travel with a group or reputable tour operator: If you are a tourist, it's generally safer to travel with a group or a reputable tour operator, especially if you are unfamiliar with the country or do not speak Arabic.

Use trusted transportation: Use registered taxis or ride-sharing apps for transportation. Avoid accepting rides from strangers or unregistered drivers.

Monitor local news: Stay informed about local news and events to be aware of any potential security concerns or public gatherings that could affect your travel plans.

Transportation

When traveling or living in Saudi Arabia, it's important to familiarize yourself with the various transportation options available to ensure a smooth and comfortable experience. Here are some tips to help you navigate the transportation system in Saudi Arabia:

Public transportation: While public transportation in Saudi Arabia is limited compared to some other countries, major cities like Riyadh and Jeddah have bus networks. Buses are generally affordable, but they might not be the most convenient or comfortable option, especially during peak hours.

Taxis: Taxis are widely available in Saudi Arabia, particularly in larger cities. Make sure to use registered taxis, identifiable by their official colours and markings. It's a good idea to negotiate the fare before starting your journey or ask the driver to use the meter to avoid overcharging.

Ride-hailing apps: Popular ride-hailing apps like Uber and Careem operate in major cities and are often a more convenient option than traditional taxis. These apps offer the advantage of predetermined fares, and you can track your journey in real-time.

Car rentals: Renting a car can provide greater flexibility and freedom, particularly if you plan to explore areas outside major cities. International and local car rental companies are available at airports and city centers. Keep in mind that you'll need a valid driver's license and may need an International Driving Permit (IDP) from your home country.

Intercity travel: For intercity travel, the Saudi Railways Organization (SRO) operates train services between Riyadh, Dammam, and Al-Qassim. The Haramain High-Speed Railway connects Mecca, Medina, Jeddah, and King Abdullah Economic City. For long-distance travel within the country, the Saudi Public Transport Company (SAPTCO) operates bus services between major cities.

Air travel: Domestic flights are a fast and convenient option for traveling long distances within Saudi Arabia. Major airlines, such as Saudi Arabian Airlines (Saudia) and Flynas, offer regular flights between major cities.

Abide by traffic rules: Driving in Saudi Arabia can be challenging due to heavy traffic and sometimes aggressive driving habits. Always follow traffic rules, wear seat belts, and avoid using mobile phones while driving. Be cautious and patient on the road.

Women drivers: Since 2018, women are allowed to drive in Saudi Arabia. Female expats and visitors with valid driving licenses from their home countries can obtain a temporary Saudi driving license or use an International Driving Permit (IDP).

Be mindful of prayer times: During daily prayer times, most businesses, including gas stations, close for a short period. Plan your travel around these times to avoid delays.

Accommodation

Finding suitable accommodation is an important aspect of living or traveling in Saudi Arabia. Here are some tips to help you find a comfortable and convenient place to stay:

Hotels: Saudi Arabia has a wide range of hotels, from budget options to luxury establishments. International hotel chains, as well as locally owned hotels, are available in major cities. It is advisable to book your hotel in advance, especially during peak seasons or religious events like Hajj and Umrah when accommodations are in high demand.

Serviced apartments: Serviced apartments can be a good option for longer stays or for travellers looking for more space and privacy. They usually come with fully equipped kitchens, living areas, and amenities like laundry facilities and Wi-Fi. Some serviced apartments are also part of hotel complexes, offering additional services like housekeeping, room service, and access to hotel facilities.

Short-term rentals: Platforms like Airbnb, Booking.com, and local websites offer short-term rental options, such as apartments or villas. This can be a cost-effective and flexible alternative to hotels, especially for families or larger groups. Always read reviews and check the location before booking a short-term rental.

Compounds: For expats planning to live in Saudi Arabia, residential compounds are a popular choice. Compounds offer a gated community living experience with various amenities like swimming pools, gyms, and supermarkets. They provide a secure environment and often have a more relaxed atmosphere than living outside a compound. It's essential to research different compounds and choose one that meets your needs and preferences.

Real estate agents: When looking for long-term housing, consider working with a reputable local real estate agent to help you find the most suitable accommodation. They can provide valuable insights into the local market, assist with negotiations, and help you navigate the rental process.

Negotiate the rent: In some cases, you might be able to negotiate the rent, especially for long-term stays. Don't be afraid to discuss the price with your landlord or real estate agent.

Understand your lease: Before signing a lease or rental agreement, make sure to read and understand all the terms and conditions. Ask for clarification on any unclear points, and ensure the contract includes any agreed-upon terms.

Location: Choose a location that is convenient for your needs, such as proximity to work, schools, public transportation, and amenities. Keep in mind that some neighbourhoods may have restrictions on renting to single men or women or may cater specifically to certain nationalities.

Healthcare

Healthcare is an important consideration for travellers and expats in Saudi Arabia. Here are some tips to help ensure you have access to quality healthcare during your stay:

Public and private healthcare: Saudi Arabia has both public and private healthcare facilities. While public hospitals provide free or low-cost healthcare to citizens, expats may need to use private facilities, which generally offer a higher standard of care and shorter wait times. It is essential to understand which hospitals and clinics cater to expats in your area.

Health insurance: It is mandatory for expats working in Saudi Arabia to have health insurance provided by their employer. For travellers, it is highly recommended to obtain comprehensive travel health insurance before arrival, covering emergency medical treatment, evacuation, and repatriation.

Find a reliable doctor: Research and identify a reliable primary care physician and any necessary specialists in your area. Seek recommendations from friends, colleagues, or online expat forums. Make sure the doctor is familiar with treating expats and speaks a language you are comfortable with.

Medications: If you require prescription medication, bring an adequate supply with you, or ensure you can obtain it in Saudi Arabia. Bring a copy of your prescription and a letter from your doctor explaining the medication and its necessity. Be aware that some medications may be restricted or unavailable in Saudi Arabia.

Vaccinations: Before traveling to Saudi Arabia, consult your doctor to ensure your vaccinations are up to date. Some vaccinations, like meningococcal and polio, are required for travellers entering the country for Hajj and Umrah. It is also recommended to have routine vaccinations such as hepatitis A, hepatitis B, and typhoid.

Emergency care: Familiarize yourself with emergency medical services and the location of the nearest hospital or clinic. In case of an emergency, call 997 for an ambulance.

Preventive measures: Take preventive measures to maintain your health, such as drinking bottled water, practicing good hygiene, avoiding undercooked or uncooked foods, and using mosquito repellents to prevent vector-borne diseases.

Dental care: Dental care in Saudi Arabia is generally of good quality, particularly in private clinics. If you need dental treatment, seek recommendations for a reputable dentist from friends, colleagues, or online expat forums.

Mental health: Mental healthcare services may be limited in Saudi Arabia, particularly for non-Arabic speakers. If you require mental health support, it may be helpful to find a therapist or counsellor who can provide remote services in your preferred language.

18. OVERCOMING STEREOTYPES AND PREJUDICES

Promoting understanding and respect in a culturally diverse environment such as Saudi Arabia requires effort, empathy, and open-mindedness. Here are some strategies for overcoming stereotypes and prejudices:

Educate yourself: Learn about Saudi Arabian history, culture, and customs. Familiarize yourself with local values, beliefs, and practices to develop a better understanding of the people you interact with. Read books, attend cultural events, and engage in conversations with locals to deepen your knowledge.

Challenge your assumptions: Recognize that stereotypes and prejudices are often rooted in assumptions and misinformation. Be aware of your biases and actively work to challenge them. Reflect on your beliefs and question their validity.

Practice empathy: Put yourself in others' shoes and try to understand their perspectives, experiences, and feelings. Empathy is key to building connections and fostering mutual respect.

Engage in open dialogue: Engage in open, respectful conversations with people from different backgrounds. Share your experiences and ask questions to learn more about others. Be prepared to listen and learn, even if the conversation is challenging.

Show respect: Treat everyone with kindness and respect, regardless of their background. Acknowledge cultural differences and be sensitive to others' feelings and beliefs. Respect local customs and traditions and try to adapt your behaviour accordingly.

Avoid generalizations: Be mindful of the language you use and avoid making sweeping generalizations about people based on their nationality, religion, or culture. Recognize that individuals are unique and should not be defined solely by their cultural background.

Seek diverse perspectives: Actively seek out and engage with people from different backgrounds to broaden your understanding of the world. Surrounding yourself with diverse perspectives will help you challenge your own beliefs and prejudices.

Encourage others: Share your learnings and experiences with friends, family, and colleagues. Encourage others to educate themselves about different cultures and challenge their own biases.

Be patient: Overcoming stereotypes and prejudices is a long-term process that requires patience and persistence. Recognize that change takes time and continue to make a conscious effort to promote understanding and respect in your interactions with others.

19. BUILDING CROSS-CULTURAL RELATIONSHIPS

Building cross-cultural relationships in a diverse environment like Saudi Arabia requires understanding, patience, and flexibility. Here are some tips for effective communication, conflict resolution, and collaboration across cultures:

Learn the language: Try to learn some basic phrases in Arabic, the official language of Saudi Arabia. This will demonstrate your interest in the culture and facilitate communication with locals.

Understand cultural differences: Familiarize yourself with cultural norms, values, and customs in Saudi Arabia. This will help you avoid misunderstandings and foster mutual respect.

Adapt your communication style: Be aware that communication styles can differ across cultures. In Saudi Arabia, people may value indirect and polite communication. Be mindful of your tone, body language, and expressions to ensure your message is well-received.

Practice active listening: Listen carefully to what others are saying and show that you are genuinely interested in their perspective. Ask clarifying questions and paraphrase their statements to ensure you understand their point of view.

Be patient and flexible: Building cross-cultural relationships takes time and effort. Be patient and open to adjusting your behaviour and expectations based on the cultural context.

Address conflicts proactively: If conflicts arise, address them promptly and openly. Maintain a respectful and open-minded attitude and focus on finding a solution that benefits all parties involved.

Seek common ground: Identify shared goals, values, and interests to build rapport and foster collaboration. Emphasize the importance of working together to achieve common objectives.

Show appreciation and respect: Express gratitude for others' contributions and acknowledge their achievements. Show respect for their opinions, even if they differ from your own.

Encourage open dialogue: Create an environment where everyone feels comfortable sharing their thoughts, ideas, and concerns. Encourage open communication and foster a culture of trust and inclusiveness.

Participate in cultural activities: Immerse yourself in local cultural events and activities to deepen your understanding of Saudi Arabian customs and traditions. This will also provide opportunities to meet new people and expand your network.

20. ADAPTING TO CULTURAL DIFFERENCES

Adapting to cultural differences can be challenging for foreigners living and working in Saudi Arabia. However, with patience, respect, and an open mind, you can successfully navigate this unique cultural environment. Here are some tips for adapting to life in Saudi Arabia:

Learn the language: Acquiring basic Arabic language skills will help you communicate more effectively with locals and show respect for their culture.

Familiarize yourself with customs and traditions: Before arriving in Saudi Arabia, research its customs, traditions, and social norms. This will help you avoid misunderstandings and show respect for the local culture.

Dress conservatively: Dress modestly in public, especially in religious and cultural settings. For women, this typically means wearing an abaya and a headscarf, while men should wear long pants and avoid sleeveless shirts.

Be aware of gender segregation: In many public places, gender segregation is still common. Respect these norms and follow local guidelines regarding interactions between men and women.

Understand the role of religion: Islam plays a central role in Saudi Arabian society. Be respectful of Islamic practices, such as daily prayers and fasting during Ramadan.

Respect local laws and regulations: Familiarize yourself with Saudi Arabian laws and adhere to them. This includes restrictions on alcohol consumption, public displays of affection, and photography of certain sites.

Build relationships: Networking and building relationships with locals can be invaluable in helping you adjust to life in Saudi Arabia. Join clubs, attend social events, and participate in cultural activities to meet new people and learn about the culture firsthand.

Be patient and adaptable: Adjusting to a new culture takes time. Remain patient and flexible as you navigate cultural differences and adapt to your new environment.

Seek support from other expats: Connect with other expats living in Saudi Arabia who can offer advice, insights, and companionship as you adjust to your new surroundings.

Maintain a sense of humour: Embrace the challenges and enjoy the unique experiences that come with living and working in a foreign country. A sense of humour can help you cope with difficult situations and make your time in Saudi Arabia more enjoyable.

21. DEVELOPING CULTURAL INTELLIGENCE

Developing cultural intelligence is essential for fostering effective communication, empathy, and understanding when living or working in a foreign country like Saudi Arabia. Cultural intelligence refers to one's ability to recognize, understand, and adapt to the cultural differences of others. It involves being aware of one's own cultural perspective and how it impacts interactions with people from different backgrounds. Here are some strategies for developing cultural intelligence in the context of Saudi Arabia:

Educate yourself: Learn about the history, customs, values, and beliefs of Saudi Arabian culture. This will give you a foundation for understanding the cultural context and perspectives of locals.

Learn the language: Developing basic Arabic language skills can greatly improve your ability to communicate and understand the nuances of Saudi Arabian culture.

Engage with locals: Interact with Saudi Arabians through social, professional, and cultural events. This will help you learn about their perspectives and experiences and build meaningful relationships.

Observe and ask questions: Pay attention to the behaviour and communication styles of locals and ask questions to gain a better understanding of the cultural context behind their actions.

Develop empathy: Put yourself in the shoes of Saudi Arabians and try to understand their perspectives and emotions. This will help you appreciate their experiences and create a deeper connection.

Be open-minded and non-judgmental: Recognize that your own cultural values and beliefs may not be universal. Approach unfamiliar customs and practices with curiosity and respect, rather than judgment.

Adapt your behaviour: Adjust your communication style, body language, and actions to align with the cultural norms and expectations of Saudi Arabian society. This demonstrates respect and facilitates more effective interactions.

Reflect on your experiences: Regularly evaluate your interactions and experiences in Saudi Arabia to identify areas where you can improve your cultural intelligence.

Learn from mistakes: Mistakes are inevitable when navigating a new culture. Acknowledge and learn from them, using these experiences to grow your cultural intelligence.

Seek feedback: Solicit feedback from locals and other expats on your cultural understanding and adaptability. This can help you identify areas for improvement and develop strategies for enhancing your cultural intelligence.

22. CASE STUDIES AND REAL LIFE EXAMPLES

Building trust in business: A foreign business executive was tasked with negotiating a deal with a Saudi Arabian company. Initially, the executive focused solely on the business aspects and failed to develop personal relationships with their Saudi counterparts. They soon realized that trust and personal connections were crucial in Saudi business culture. The executive began to engage in small talk and attend social events, ultimately building trust and successfully closing the deal.

Dress code adaptation: A female expatriate working in Saudi Arabia initially felt uncomfortable with the requirement to wear an abaya and headscarf in public. Over time, she learned to appreciate the cultural significance of these garments and found that adapting her dress code helped her integrate better into Saudi society and gain respect from her local colleagues.

Overcoming language barriers: An international NGO worker assigned to a project in Saudi Arabia faced challenges in communicating with the local population due to the language barrier. They decided to enrol in an Arabic language course, which greatly improved their ability to understand and communicate with local communities. As a result, they were able to establish stronger relationships and work more effectively on the project.

Navigating gender dynamics: A foreign female executive visited Saudi Arabia for a series of meetings with potential clients. She researched the cultural norms and was careful to dress modestly, maintain appropriate body language, and avoid initiating physical contact with men. Her cultural awareness and sensitivity allowed her to engage effectively in meetings and forge strong business relationships.

Managing religious practices: An international company operating in Saudi Arabia faced challenges in accommodating the daily prayer times of their Muslim employees. The company adjusted work schedules to allow for prayer breaks and provided a dedicated prayer space within the office. This flexibility demonstrated respect for the local culture and significantly improved employee morale and productivity.

23. LESSONS LEARNED AND BEST PRACTICES

Strategies for Navigating Cultural Differences in Saudi Arabia

Do your homework: Before arriving in Saudi Arabia, research the country's history, customs, and traditions. Familiarizing yourself with the local culture will help you avoid unintentional offenses and misunderstandings.

Learn the language: Although many Saudis speak English, learning basic Arabic phrases can go a long way in building rapport and showing respect for the local culture.

Be respectful of Islamic practices: Islam plays a central role in Saudi Arabian life. Be mindful of prayer times, dress modestly, and adhere to restrictions on alcohol consumption and public displays of affection.

Build personal relationships: In Saudi Arabia, trust and personal relationships are crucial in both social and business settings. Invest time in getting to know your Saudi counterparts and be prepared for indirect communication styles.

Adapt to gender dynamics: Be aware of the different gender roles and expectations in Saudi society. Women should dress modestly and be mindful of physical contact with men, while men should respect the boundaries set by Saudi women.

Respect hierarchy: Saudi culture places a strong emphasis on hierarchy and status. Show respect for elders and those in positions of authority and be prepared for decision-making processes to be slower and more hierarchical than in other cultures.

Be patient and flexible: Saudi Arabia operates on a more relaxed sense of time than many Western countries. Be prepared for meetings to start late or be rescheduled and allow for additional time when planning events or projects.

Observe local customs: Participate in traditional customs, such as sharing coffee or tea, and be prepared to accept invitations to social gatherings. This will help you build rapport with your Saudi counterparts and gain a deeper understanding of the local culture.

Seek local advice: When in doubt, consult with local colleagues or friends who can provide guidance on cultural norms and expectations. They can help you navigate cultural differences and provide valuable insights into Saudi society.

Cultivate cultural intelligence: Develop empathy, flexibility, and curiosity to better understand and adapt to the Saudi culture. Being open-minded and willing to learn from local perspectives will enable you to build strong relationships and achieve success in Saudi Arabia.

24. RESOURCES AND FURTHER READING

Books

- "Saudi Arabia: A Kingdom in Peril" by Paul Aarts and Carolien Roelants
- "Princess: A True Story of Life Behind the Veil in Saudi Arabia" by Jean Sasson
- "Inside the Kingdom: My Life in Saudi Arabia" by Carmen bin Ladin
- "The House of Saud: The Rise and Rule of the Most Powerful Dynasty in the Arab World" by David Holden and Richard Johns

Articles

- "Understanding Saudi Arabia" - Harvard Business Review: https://hbr.org/2012/05/understanding-saudi-arabia
- "Navigating Saudi Arabia's Cultural Minefield" - Forbes: https://www.forbes.com/sites/iese/2013/11/25/navigating-saudi-arabias-cultural-minefield/

Websites

- Saudi Gazette (English-language news site): http://saudigazette.com.sa/
- Arab News (English-language news site): https://www.arabnews.com/
- Ministry of Culture, Kingdom of Saudi Arabia: https://www.moc.gov.sa/en/
- Saudi Arabian Cultural Mission to the USA: https://sacm.org/

Organisations

- King Abdulaziz Center for World Culture (Ithra): https://www.ithra.com/en/
- The Saudi Commission for Tourism and National Heritage: https://scth.gov.sa/en/Pages/default.aspx
- The Islamic Educational, Scientific and Cultural Organization (ISESCO): https://www.isesco.org.ma/

Language Learning

- Transparent Language: Learn Arabic online: https://www.transparent.com/learn-arabic/
- Rosetta Stone: Arabic language courses: https://www.rosettastone.com/learn-arabic/